Napoleon: A Very Short Introduction

VERY SHORT INTRODUCTIONS are for anyone wanting a stimulating and accessible way into a new subject. They are written by experts, and have been translated into more than 45 different languages.

The series began in 1995, and now covers a wide variety of topics in every discipline. The VSI library currently contains over 550 volumes—a Very Short Introduction to everything from Psychology and Philosophy of Science to American History and Relativity—and continues to grow in every subject area.

Very Short Introductions available now:

ABOLITIONISM Richard S. Newman
ACCOUNTING Christopher Nobes
ADAM SMITH Christopher J. Berry
ADOLESCENCE Peter K. Smith
ADVERTISING Winston Fletcher
AFRICAN AMERICAN RELIGION
    Eddie S. Glaude Jr
AFRICAN HISTORY John Parker and
    Richard Rathbone
AFRICAN POLITICS Ian Taylor
AFRICAN RELIGIONS
    Jacob K. Olupona
AGEING Nancy A. Pachana
AGNOSTICISM Robin Le Poidevin
AGRICULTURE Paul Brassley and
    Richard Soffe
ALEXANDER THE GREAT
    Hugh Bowden
ALGEBRA Peter M. Higgins
AMERICAN CULTURAL HISTORY
    Eric Avila
AMERICAN HISTORY Paul S. Boyer
AMERICAN IMMIGRATION
    David A. Gerber
AMERICAN LEGAL HISTORY
    G. Edward White
AMERICAN NAVAL HISTORY
    Craig L. Symonds
AMERICAN POLITICAL HISTORY
    Donald Critchlow
AMERICAN POLITICAL PARTIES
    AND ELECTIONS L. Sandy Maisel
AMERICAN POLITICS
    Richard M. Valelly

THE AMERICAN PRESIDENCY
    Charles O. Jones
THE AMERICAN REVOLUTION
    Robert J. Allison
AMERICAN SLAVERY
    Heather Andrea Williams
THE AMERICAN WEST Stephen Aron
AMERICAN WOMEN'S HISTORY
    Susan Ware
ANAESTHESIA Aidan O'Donnell
ANALYTIC PHILOSOPHY
    Michael Beaney
ANARCHISM Colin Ward
ANCIENT ASSYRIA Karen Radner
ANCIENT EGYPT Ian Shaw
ANCIENT EGYPTIAN ART AND
    ARCHITECTURE Christina Riggs
ANCIENT GREECE Paul Cartledge
THE ANCIENT NEAR EAST
    Amanda H. Podany
ANCIENT PHILOSOPHY Julia Annas
ANCIENT WARFARE
    Harry Sidebottom
ANGELS David Albert Jones
ANGLICANISM Mark Chapman
THE ANGLO-SAXON AGE John Blair
ANIMAL BEHAVIOUR
    Tristram D. Wyatt
THE ANIMAL KINGDOM
    Peter Holland
ANIMAL RIGHTS David DeGrazia
THE ANTARCTIC Klaus Dodds
ANTHROPOCENE Erle C. Ellis
ANTISEMITISM Steven Beller

Available soon:

For more information visit our web site

www.oup.com/vsi/

David A. Bell

NAPOLEON

A Very Short Introduction

OXFORD
UNIVERSITY PRESS

OXFORD
UNIVERSITY PRESS

Oxford University Press is a department of the University of Oxford.
It furthers the University's objective of excellence in research, scholarship,
and education by publishing worldwide. Oxford is a registered trade mark of
Oxford University Press in the UK and certain other countries.

Published in the United States of America by Oxford University Press
198 Madison Avenue, New York, NY 10016, United States of America.

Library of Congress Cataloging-in-Publication Data
Names: Bell, David A. (David Avrom) author.
Title: Napoleon : a very short introduction / David A. Bell.
Description: New York : Oxford University Press, 2018. |
Series: Very short introductions | "First published in hardback
as Napoleon: A Concise Biography, 2015." |
Includes bibliographical references and index.
Identifiers: LCCN 2018018296 (print) |
LCCN 2018020848 (ebook) | ISBN 9780199321674 (updf) |
ISBN 9780199321681 (epub) | ISBN 9780190911959 (online component) |
ISBN 9780199321667 (paperback)
Subjects: LCSH: Napoleon I, Emperor of the French, 1769-1821. |
Emperors—France—Biography. | France—History—1789-1815. |
BISAC: HISTORY / General. | HISTORY / Europe / France. |
HISTORY / Modern / 18th Century.
Classification: LCC DC203 (ebook) | LCC DC203 .B44 2018 (print) |
DDC 944.05092 [B] —dc23
LC record available at https://lccn.loc.gov/2018018296

Printed by Integrated Books International, United States of America
on acid-free paper

For Paul and Judith Farber

Contents

List of illustrations

Preface

It is hardly surprising that over the past two centuries, Napoleon Bonaparte has attracted legions of biographers. His life was enormously important, endlessly fascinating, and connected to some of the most controversial and constantly reinterpreted events in world history—first and foremost, the French Revolution. It was also so extraordinarily well-documented a life that each successive biographer can usually manage to find and highlight some significant fact, observation, or remark that predecessors have neglected. Between 1995 and 2015, the lure of bicentennial celebrations provided an additional incentive to would-be biographers, and the results have threatened to collapse many a bookshelf.

Why, then, this book? I can offer two answers. First, and most obviously, while the current crop of biographies has many virtues, concision is not among them. Philip Dwyer's two-volume study weighs in at some 1,650 pages. The first part of Patrice Gueniffey's planned two volumes comes to nearly 1,000—and takes the story only up to 1802! Even Steven Englund's relatively svelte contribution still stretches over 575 pages. (See the further reading list for more details on these works.) Not only do many readers not have the time and patience for such tomes, but it is all too easy to get lost in the welter of details—especially for readers without formal training in the history of the period. Gueniffey's authoritative study, written for French readers, takes for granted a detailed knowledge of the events of the French Revolution. My book has been written for readers who want an accurate, readable portrait of Napoleon that incorporates the results of recent research but is also concise and is accessible to those without specialized knowledge.

But it is in no sense a simple summary or synthesis of earlier work. I have incorporated much original research drawn from my own scholarly work on the French revolutionary and Napoleonic periods, and I have brought to bear insights drawn from that work. The result, while not a full-scale reinterpretation of Napoleon, nonetheless offers a new perspective on his life, his rule, and his relation to the age of revolutions. As will be seen, I argue that the immense political upheaval of the French Revolution, and the emergence of newly intense forms of European warfare, reinforced each other in a strikingly powerful and original manner that made Napoleon possible. He, in turn, tried—and ultimately failed—to forge a regime that based its legitimacy on the revolutionary principles of popular sovereignty and civic equality, but also on personal charisma and military glory.

I am grateful to Nancy Toff at Oxford University Press for first proposing this book to me, for her famously expert editing, and for guiding the book smoothly through the publication process. Rafe Blaufarb and Steve Englund (whose own brilliantly written biography of Napoleon was an inspiration) kindly read through the draft manuscript and provided many useful suggestions and corrections, as did the press's two anonymous readers. I could not have written this book, in the midst of a very busy period of life, without the love and support of my wife, Donna Farber, and of our children, Elana and Joseph. The book is dedicated to Donna's parents, Paul and Judith Farber, in gratitude for having welcomed me so warmly into their family for so many years.

Introduction

March 7, 1815. Laffrey, Department of the Isère, France.

It is cold, in late winter, here in the foothills of the Alps, and the open plain by the side of a lake offers no shelter from the wind. But for the two groups of French soldiers facing each other, the weather is the last thing on their minds. They are, for the most part, army veterans of long standing, and they know all too well the horrors of the battlefield—know all too well that within minutes they could be dead, or screaming in agony from ghastly wounds. On one side stand eight hundred members of France's Fifth Infantry Regiment, who owe obedience to His Majesty, Louis XVIII of the House of Bourbon, King of France and Navarre. On the other are a slightly larger number of men, dirty, tired and hungry, who have spent the past week marching more than two hundred miles north from the Mediterranean coast, and who have the seemingly absurd ambition of making it all the way to Paris and seizing control of the country. Their chances of success would appear minimal, no reason at all to risk dying in this picturesque but otherwise forgettable spot. But they have one enormous advantage. He is in their midst, wearing an old gray army jacket, of average height, with thinning hair and a pronounced paunch, speaking French with a thick Corsican accent. He is the man that all the men on the field, from both sides, had once sworn to die for: Napoleon Bonaparte.

It has been the better part of a year since Napoleon fell from power, but the French, and Europeans more generally, are having a hard time forgetting him. He is, after all, the man who, born in obscurity, acquired the greatest military reputation of any European military commander in centuries while still in his twenties. At thirty he ruled France, and at forty he dominated Europe as no individual had since Charlemagne—perhaps, indeed, since the Caesars. The wars he fought had changed the map of Europe forever and left millions of its inhabitants in early graves. But his fall had been as spectacular and swift as his rise, and his forty-fifth birthday, in August 1814, saw him in exile on the tiny Italian island of Elba and replaced in Paris by the Bourbon dynasty that the French Revolution had toppled more than twenty years before.

And then, on February 26, Napoleon and his followers escaped from Elba by boat, landing three days later on the French coast near Cannes. They have marched north peacefully, despite the protests of some local officials. But now, in Laffrey, they are facing a battalion of King Louis's army, backed by thousands more soldiers close by in the city of Grenoble. It seems as if their adventure may quickly come to a blood-soaked end.

As the armies face each other, indecisively, the royalist battalion commander steps forward. "If you do not withdraw," he shouts hesitantly to Napoleon, "you will be arrested." On both sides, hands nervously clutch loaded muskets.

But then Napoleon orders his own men to lower their weapons. An aide protests, but he insists. He steps forward, out in front of his own troops, to within twenty feet of the royalist regiment. "Soldiers of the Fifth!" he cries out to them. "I am your emperor! Acknowledge me!" He walks a few more steps, and in a dramatic gesture, opens his coat, exposing his chest as a target. "If there is any soldier among you who wants to kill his emperor," he continues, his voice firm, "here I am!"

For a moment, there is silence. Then, somewhere in the royalist lines, a voice can be heard ordering men to open fire. But no one does. The line stands, fearful, indecisive. And then, a different cry is heard. "Vive l'Empereur!" "Long Live the Emperor!" A single voice at first, but immediately repeated by others. "Vive l'Empereur!" In a moment, the entire royalist battalion is shouting the words, and as they do, they throw down their weapons, surround Napoleon joyously, and rush to embrace the men who have come with him from Elba. Hardened soldiers burst into tears as they clasp each other, screaming deliriously, "Vive l'Empereur!" As the clamor subsides, Napoleon smiles contentedly at his small army, which has just doubled in size. He prepares to move onward, further north.

1. Royalist troops at Laffrey rally to the side of Napoleon Bonaparte, who has just escaped from exile in Elba and is marching on Paris in March 1815. This is how the painter Carl von Steuben later imagined the scene.

Twelve days later, in the middle of the night, Louis XVIII will flee Paris. A few hours after that, Napoleon Bonaparte, cheered by wildly enthusiastic crowds, followed by a hugely swollen army of supporters, will reclaim his capital city. His renewed rule will be famously short—the episode goes by the title "the Hundred Days"—and will end soon after the disastrous battle of Waterloo, Napoleon's greatest defeat. But his legend, massively amplified by the episode, will survive.

The "encounter at Laffrey" stands as one of the most dramatic moments in one of the most dramatic lives anyone has ever lived. It was also, to an extent that historians have not always recognized, stage-managed. One of Napoleon's officers had met with a royalist officer before the confrontation, and the royalist had confessed that his men would probably refuse to fire on their former sovereign. Napoleon's envoy then suggested, with a crowd of royalist soldiers listening in, that Napoleon could make a personal appeal. While the emperor could not know for sure that the royalists would hold their fire, when he opened his coat on the afternoon of March 7, he did so with reasonable confidence that his gesture would have the intended effect.

This stage-management is, in its own way, as important as the drama itself for understanding Napoleon's life. From his first campaigns in the mid-1790s, he knew the political importance of actively crafting his image in all available media: print, painting, sculpture, oratory, even architecture. It is no coincidence that so many images of the man have achieved iconic status. There is the triumphant young general atop a rearing horse in the Alps, the bold emperor seizing a crown from the pope and setting it on his own head in Notre Dame Cathedral, the strutting, mature leader with the ultrafamiliar gesture: hand thrust into his vest over his stomach. Napoleon crafted all these images quite deliberately. He was a product of the first great modern age of celebrity, and he understood, viscerally, how to manage celebrity in the service of power. In the voluminous source material that has survived about him, a very high proportion bears the marks of his own conscious manipulation and design.

It is vital to understand this point about Napoleon Bonaparte from the start, because it is all too easy to see him as a pure force—and freak—of nature who imposed himself on the world through sheer boldness and brilliance. Bold and brilliant he was, but also shrewd. He understood how radically Europe had changed in the decades during which he had come of age, and he knew better than anyone else how to seize the new opportunities that had arisen. While he did, repeatedly, take enormous and dramatic risks, in his battles, in his grand strategy, and in politics, he also did everything possible to maximize the odds in his favor.

The story of Napoleon's life runs from his birth on Corsica in 1769 to his death in final exile on a much smaller island, Saint Helena, in 1821, and stretches beyond his death to include the posthumous battles over his reputation. It is the story of a man with genuinely extraordinary personal qualities, and it involves some of the most dramatic events in history. It spans the construction of institutions that even today remain enormously influential in France and beyond, but also actions that resulted in enormous human devastation. But it is a story that cannot be understood without placing Napoleon in the broader context of his age—both the historical changes that made him possible and the historical forces that he so powerfully grasped hold of. So before transporting the scene to the Corsican town of Ajaccio, where Napoleon came into the world in 1769, I must first say a few words about what historians call the age of democratic revolutions, and revolutionary war.

With all due respect to Thomas Jefferson, in the year Napoleon was born, few truths seemed less evident to most Europeans than the idea that all men were created equal, and endowed by their creator with unalienable rights to life, liberty, and the pursuit of happiness. In 1766, the king of France, Louis XV, had appeared before the magistrates of his highest court of law and declared: "Sovereign power resides in my person alone…to me alone belongs legislative power without subordination and undivided… the rights and interests of the nation…repose solely in my hands." In practice, European kings did not possess the sort of dictatorial power such words conjure up today. They generally felt obliged to respect precedent and to cooperate with political institutions such as local estates and courts. Nonetheless, they did not believe their subjects possessed any sort of natural liberty, and very few of the subjects themselves claimed it. France in particular had no elected parliament, no freedom of speech or religion, no habeas corpus or jury trials, and no protections against unreasonable search and seizure or cruel punishment. Physical torture was an established part of legal procedure.

Still less did Europeans see each other as social equals. In every European state, steep social hierarchies were engrained in law, separating nobles from commoners and clerics from laity and subdividing every order of the state into a myriad of smaller orders, corporate bodies, and guilds, each with its own distinct privileges. "In every part of the state," French magistrates told the king in 1776, "there exist bodies which can be regarded as links in a great chain, the first link of which is in the hands of Your Majesty." France, like many other European states, was a slaveholding empire that relied for much of its prosperity on cash crops produced in overseas colonies by a brutal system of coerced African labor. In 1789, France's Caribbean colonies contained as many slaves as the entire United States.

Nor did the pursuit of earthly happiness strike most Europeans as any sort of birthright. Every European state possessed an established church. The Christian churches taught that terrestrial life was a vale of tears, and that men and women should look for happiness only in the eternal life they would enjoy after death. And the churches taught submission: "Render therefore unto Caesar the things which are Caesar's" (Matthew 22); "For there is no power but of God: the powers that be are ordained of God. Whosoever therefore resisteth the power…shall receive to themselves damnation" (Romans 13). In Catholic Europe, very much including France, the Catholic Church possessed vast landholdings, wealth, and political power.

If, by the 1770s, some Europeans had come to share Jefferson's revolutionary convictions about natural rights, the phenomenon had complex origins and took complex forms. The European Enlightenment was more a moment than a movement, still less an organized movement, and its most prominent thinkers argued endlessly among themselves. Most of them shared a general commitment to freedom of thought and religious toleration, and a general commitment to the rule of reason and utility in human affairs, but they could not agree about how these ideals should be implemented or about the best form of government. Nor did any of them imagine the upheaval that was approaching. In 1762, one of the most important, Jean-Jacques Rousseau, did write, "We are on the edge of a revolution." But by this word he meant a sudden, uncontrollable, and catastrophic crisis, not a long-term political transformation, possessing its own logic and its own governing ideals. Rousseau speculated brilliantly about the form a truly democratic regime might take but in the same breath declared that European states had grown too aged and decadent to undertake the experiment—with one striking exception: Corsica. "I have a presentiment," he wrote, "that this little island will one day astonish Europe."

Even as the Enlightenment philosophers debated, a host of social and cultural developments were putting pressure on long-standing justifications of power and privilege from other directions. Economic prosperity, driven by colonial trade, by a physical climate that had warmed since the previous century's "little ice age," and in some areas by the early stirrings of modern industry, led to the expansion of cities, and in them a profusion of consumer goods. While a self-conscious "middle class" had yet to coalesce, new hierarchies of wealth and consumption were arising that did not align easily with the older hierarchies of noble and commoner. Among the most important consumer items were books, which an increasingly literate population read in greater numbers than ever. These books transmitted everything from advanced philosophical thought to crude pornography that often depicted kings, queens, and clerics in embarrassing positions. Even more important, though, was that classic eighteenth-century literary genre the novel, often written in the form of letters between people, especially women, of humble birth. The best-selling novels of the period, along with much of the dramatic literature and visual art, had highly sentimental, even melodramatic plots and messages. They encouraged readers and viewers to feel sympathy for characters deliberately portrayed as ordinary, as opposed to princes and heroes. They were also intensely moralizing, inculcating a deep hostility toward selfishness, corruption, and frivolity while praising selflessness and patriotic virtue.

In Britain, these changes helped fuel a national dynamism that propelled the country, aided by its powerful navy and a robust financial system, to triumph in imperial wars. In France, these changes had much the opposite effect. A dysfunctional government proved largely incapable of translating economic dynamism into higher tax revenues, even as a series of ruinously expensive wars drained the treasury. Royal attempts to increase taxes on the privileged classes led to paralyzing protests, despite the king's claim to absolute power. Ever more dependent on international lending to keep itself afloat, by the end of the 1780s the French state was on the brink of catastrophe. And then, during a sharp economic downturn, it went over the edge.

In 1788, the young and hesitant King Louis XVI convoked a national body, the Estates General, that had not met since 1615, to deal with the financial crisis. The leaders of the "Third Estate" (the commoners), who no longer felt automatic subservience to crown and nobility, and who were inspired at least in part by the example of the American Revolution, demanded a greater share of representation than the system had traditionally accorded them. In June 1789 the king gave in to their requests, but the combination of political turmoil and popular misery had already turned explosive. On July 14, Parisian crowds fearful of a royal coup d'état against the new "National Assembly" stormed the royal fortress and prison known as the Bastille. Across France, insurgent urban politicians took over municipalities, while bands of peasants attacked noble châteaux. In a summer of revolutionary fear and exultation, the Assembly proclaimed the abolition of "feudal" privileges and drafted the stirring Declaration of the Rights of Man and Citizen. In October, Parisian crowds led by market women marched on the royal palace of Versailles, outside Paris, and forced the royal family and Assembly to move to the capital. The French Revolution had begun.

For two years, the Assembly tried to find a way to preserve a constitutional monarchy while beginning to implement a vastly ambitious reform program. But the more enthusiastic supporters of reform quickly fell out with conservatives, and with the king himself, over issues that included the extent of the suffrage and whether the Catholic Church should be subordinated to the state. In 1791 the royal family was caught trying to flee the country, and while Louis XVI returned to Paris and remained chief executive, opposition to the monarchy swelled. In August 1792, well-armed National Guardsmen, allied with radicalized Parisian crowds, overcame the king's guards in a pitched battle in the heart of Paris. A republic was declared, and a new Constitutional Convention took office, elected (for the first time in European history) by universal manhood suffrage. Its first great action was to put Louis XVI on trial, find him guilty, and put him to death with the new, horror-inducing decapitation machine known as the guillotine.

From this moment, the Revolution veered left at a vertiginous pace and turned increasingly violent. Another popular insurrection in 1793 led to the expulsion of so-called "Girondin" deputies from the Convention and the adoption of ambitious social policies, including price controls. A coterie of deputies around the stern, moralistic Maximilien Robespierre presided over what historians call the Reign of Terror, in which tens of thousands of alleged counterrevolutionaries went to the guillotine. Large areas of the country rose up in revolt against the Convention, leading to a series of civil wars in which hundreds of thousands more died. The Convention and its agents suppressed much Christian worship, instituted a new, non-Christian calendar, and developed utopian plans for universal education, social welfare, and the "regeneration" of the French nation. Finally, in July 1794, frightened deputies carried out a coup against Robespierre and his allies, who went to the guillotine in their turn. The Terror came to an end.

The events of this first stage of the French Revolution damaged the country in some ways. But they also swept aside social privilege and inefficient state institutions and engendered new ideas and practices of national sovereignty and civic equality. With the coming of elections and a raucous free press, political figures learned to appeal directly to ordinary citizens to gain power. The radical demagogue Jean-Paul Marat was only the most prominent revolutionary who used the printing press to forge intense bonds of attachment with his followers. As a result of all these changes, the Revolution made possible an unprecedented concentration of political authority, as well as unprecedented ways of mobilizing the country's human and material resources. In this respect, Napoleon Bonaparte would reap what the revolutionaries had sown.

Just as the Revolution radically changed the nature of politics, it also radically changed the nature of war. At the time of Napoleon's birth, European warfare had, by the horrific standards of previous centuries, turned remarkably limited. While kings and princes fought each other for territory and commercial advantage, they did not generally seek to overthrow each other's regimes. While major battles involved dreadful carnage, including the deaths of as many as a quarter of the participants, major battles were rare. "I am not at all for battles," wrote one well-known strategist and commander in the 1740s, "and I am convinced that a skillful general can go all his life without being forced to fight one." Generals preferred elaborate chess games of maneuver and siege to direct confrontation. And while civilians suffered from war, often quite dreadfully, they still probably suffered less than in any other period of European conflict. The aristocrats who dominated the officer corps in every major army subscribed to strict codes of honor that, while not always observed, did push them to respect civilian populations and to keep strict control over their men.

With the soldiers' bright uniforms and well-choreographed marching, accompanied by drum, fife, and even bagpipe music, battlefields in some ways seemed an extension of Europe's well-mannered royal courts. As one of the early French revolutionaries put it, "no longer is it nations that fight each other, but just armies and professionals; wars are like games of chance in which no one risks his all; what was once a wild rage is now just a folly." Wars could prove massively expensive, but the chief source of rising costs was their newly global scale, especially between the British and French colonial empires, and the need for ever larger navies.

During the late eighteenth century, some of the period's most creative thinkers had predicted—or even advocated—an end to this supposedly "polite" form of war. The French strategist Count Guibert predicted that if a free and virtuous nation were to arise in the midst of Europe, "its style of war will not be the one practiced by states today.... Terrible in its wrath, it will bring fire and steel to its enemy's hearth." The German philosopher Immanuel Kant, better known for his *Project for Perpetual Peace*, wrote that "the sublime needs violence.... War itself has something sublime in it,...while a long peace generally brings...low selfishness, cowardice, and effeminacy."

It took the French Revolution, however, for a new form of war actually to emerge. The new regime in France did not initially seek to impose its principles on its neighbors. But as the political conflicts in the country sharpened, a growing stream of conservatives—including much of the largely noble officer corps—fled abroad and started plotting to restore the Old Regime. The Austrian Empire, ruled by the brother of France's queen Marie-Antoinette, provided support, for them, and so did its ally Prussia. Both states loudly expressed their own concerns about the direction in which French affairs were moving. In the unsettled winter of 1791–92, French radicals in turn pushed for war in the hope of strengthening their own political position, and they found surprising support from the king and queen, who hoped foreign intervention could rescue them from their own people. In April 1792, war began.

At first it went badly for France. But at the crucial battle of Valmy, on September 20, 1792, the French managed to push back a Prussian invasion. An army swollen by inexperienced but enthusiastic revolutionaries gradually developed into a strong fighting force, and over the course of 1792 and 1793 the revolutionary government began to draw on one of France's greatest strategic advantages, its population. The country's 28 million people made it the largest in Europe, but the limited warfare of the Old Regime had never fully exploited this resource. In August 1793, the so-called mass levy formally placed all French people at the disposal of the armed forces. "The young men will fight; married men will forge weapons and transport supplies; women will make tents and uniforms and serve in hospitals; children will turn old linen into lint; old men will...rouse the courage of those who fight." Initially, hordes of poorly trained and poorly equipped draftees did more harm than good on the battlefield, and in 1793 the foreign enemies could also count on many allies within France as civil war flared. The numbers of France's foreign enemies increased as well, with Britain and Spain coming into the fight. Nonetheless, by the summer of 1794, a new cohort of French officers, many risen from the ranks, were learning how best to deploy an army that now dwarfed its opponents. Defeats gave way to victory, on both the foreign and domestic fronts.

Although the basic technology and tactics of war remained what they had been for a century—cannon firing solid projectiles, lines and columns of infantry with unwieldy and inaccurate muskets and bayonets, cavalry with swords and pistols—the revolutionary conflicts nonetheless broke strikingly from the Old Regime style of war. The French revolutionaries not only knew their own survival was at stake but quickly proclaimed as their goal nothing less than a crusade to liberate humanity. The radical Charles-Philippe Ronsin called for a "war of purification that will change the face of the world, and raise the banner of liberty over the palaces of kings, the harems of sultans,...and the temples of popes and muftis." In Britain, the conservative Edmund Burke predicted, correctly, that "the mode of civilized war will not be practiced.... The hell-hounds of war, on all sides, will be uncoupled and unmuzzled." Indeed, revolutionary generals now sought out major battles to make best use of their superior numbers, encouraged the formation of new revolutionary governments in occupied territories, and ransacked those territories to keep their own forces supplied. In the spring of 1794, the French National Convention even voted to give no quarter to British prisoners, although French commanders in the field never obeyed the order. In short, Europe was witnessing the beginnings of what some historians consider the first total war.

So in this way as well, the Revolution paved the way for Napoleon's astonishing career. Without these transformations in warfare, his own massive wars of conquest and his string of dramatic victories would have been entirely unthinkable. Napoleon was a product of total war, would become its master, and would end up its victim.

Napoleon's entire story took place against the background of the French Revolution just sketched out. "I am the French Revolution, and I will support it," Napoleon declared in 1804. His statements of this sort were almost always carefully calculated, and he often, quite blithely, contradicted himself entirely. (On another occasion he remarked: "I found the crown of France in the gutter and placed it on my head.") But when it comes to his debt to the Revolution, he spoke nothing but the truth. He certainly did not incarnate all the Revolution's principles. Indeed, many people believe that he comprehensively betrayed them. Nonetheless, the Revolution made him possible, by making possible the new forms of political authority and the new forms of war. Furthermore, these two factors powerfully reinforced each other. Napoleon built on the military successes enabled by the new forms of warfare so as to craft his political persona as a hero and savior; to inspire (at least for a time) very genuine popular support and thereby to hold power. And he exploited the new political conditions to marshal unprecedented resources to fight the wars. He was, in many ways, the keenest observer of the changes the Revolution had wrought, and he exploited them brilliantly, at least for a time.

Chapter 1
The Corsican, 1769–1796

The status of Napoleon's native Corsica, like that of Ireland, another famously unsettled European island, has wavered in history between colony, province, and independent state. Until the mid-eighteenth century, nearly everything tied Corsica to nearby Italy: language, trade, population exchanges, and politics. The Italian republic of Genoa ruled it greedily but distantly, while real power belonged to a series of powerful extended families, including, in a relatively subordinate place, the Buonapartes (the original spelling of the name). Carlo, Napoleon's father, born in 1746, was a handsome, pleasure-loving man who had trained as a lawyer in Pisa and, at just seventeen, married the fourteen-year-old daughter of another powerful clan, Letitzia Ramolini. At the time, nothing would have predicted an exceptional destiny for any of their children.

The mid-eighteenth century, however, was bringing important changes to Corsica. After several decades of revolt against the corrupt Genoese, the island established a de facto independent republic in the 1750s under the charismatic Pasquale Paoli. Then in 1768 the Kingdom of France, in order to improve its strategic position in the Mediterranean, purchased the rights over Corsica from Genoa. It sent in an occupation force, which quickly drove Paoli into exile, and introduced the more intrusive French style of administration. Carlo Buonaparte, although an ally of Paoli, decided to remain in Corsica and make his peace with the new overlords. France was alien to the Corsicans in its languages and customs, but as the largest and most powerful state in Europe, it also offered its new subjects many new opportunities. As the Scots philosopher David Hume observed keenly in the 1770s, "when a monarch extends his dominion by conquest, he soon learns to consider his old and new subjects on the same footing; because, in reality all his subjects are to him the same." Carlo Buonaparte took advantage of this fact and convinced the authorities to recognize the family as members of the French nobility. (His vivacious and strong-willed wife played a role here as well, perhaps even having an affair with the French governor.) The new status had important consequences for Carlo's children, including his second surviving son, Napoleon, who came into the world on August 15, 1769.

The story of Napoleon's early years is so thickly encrusted with fables peddled by even slight acquaintances as to make sorting truth from falsehood and exaggeration an almost impossible task. Was the mature emperor already visible in the defiant baby, or in the schoolboy leading playmates in an epic snowball fight? Napoleon certainly developed a strong and fraught bond with his older brother, Joseph, suggested above all by the fact that when in adulthood he married a woman christened Marie-Josèphe-Rose and known as Rose, he insisted she call herself "Joséphine." No less a psychological authority than Sigmund Freud wondered if Napoleon had a "Joseph fantasy." But we will never know the exact story. What we do know is that at age nine, in the winter of 1778–79, Napoleon left his close-knit Corsican family, dominated by his mother, for an austere military boarding school in what amounted to a foreign country. Thanks to the family's new status as French nobles, Carlo had managed to enroll him in the free public preparatory school at Brienne, in northern France, as the first step on the path to an officer's commission in the French army. Carlo took him and Joseph, who was initially destined for the priesthood, to France together.

Brienne was, by any measure, the defining experience of Napoleon's childhood. After a crash course in the French language, he spent five years at the school without once returning home. Historians have made much of the hazing he received from his fellow students on account of his accent, his fierce loyalty to Corsica, and a first name unfamiliar to French ears, which one fellow student rendered with poor wit as "paille-au-nez" (straw in the nose). Scholars have speculated endlessly about the effects of the experience on his character, and it is indeed likely that he derived considerable resilience and self-sufficiency from it, as well as a reasonably solid training in French, Latin, mathematics, drawing, fencing and dancing.

There was also another effect, less remarked on. Like countless lonely children, before and after, Napoleon found comfort and companionship in books. We do not know what he read at this earliest stage, but by adolescence the habit of intensive reading had already become deeply engrained. "I lived like a bear...always alone in my small room with my books...my only friends!" he wrote of his years as a teenage junior officer, when he was devouring novels, plays, and the most popular works of the French Enlightenment. And as a teenager he developed the ambition of becoming an author himself. He kept copious reading notes and a file of obscure words that might lend weight to his own writings. He started drafts of historical and philosophical essays and dialogues, including a fervently patriotic historical sketch of Corsica. He even wrote a few pages of a gothic novel: "He drew her hand to his neck. O horror! The countess's fingers sank into his broad wounds, and came out covered with blood." Some later French writers believed he showed real talent. "What a pity," commented Paul Valéry, "to see a mind as great as Napoleon's devoted to trivial things such as empires, historical events, the thundering of cannon and of men." Chateaubriand, more sensibly, concluded that "destiny was mute, and Napoleon should have been."

For an ambitious young man in Napoleon's position, a literary vocation made more sense than it might have seemed at first glance. In the ultrahierarchical French officer corps, a cadet from a low-ranking family in a far-flung province could expect to make a career, but not a very distinguished one. And while the young Napoleon remained fiercely attached to Corsica, continuing for many years to denounce the French as foreign occupiers and even swearing death to the "French Caesar" (this while preparing to join the Caesar's army!), before 1789 a return to Corsican independence looked entirely unlikely. But in the eighteenth century, many European military officers gained sizeable literary reputations, including Choderlos de Laclos, the author of *Dangerous Liaisons*, and the Marquis de Sade. There was nothing unusual in the young Napoleon writing to a famous figure of the late Enlightenment, the abbé Raynal, to introduce himself. ("I am not yet eighteen, but I am already a writer.") And there was nothing unusual in Raynal sending back words of fulsome encouragement.

In 1791, following a path blazed by Jean-Jacques Rousseau, Napoleon would try to jump-start a literary career by entering a prize essay contest sponsored by a learned academy, in this case on the subject of happiness. Unlike Rousseau, he did not win, but his entry represented his best piece of written work, and contained lines that, coming from one of the most ambitious men in history, appear more than a little ironic: "Ambition, like all disordered passions, is a violent and unthinking delirium.... Like a fire fed by a pitiless wind, it only burns out after having consumed everything in its path."

Yet for all his hopes of literary glory, Napoleon did not manage to complete many other manuscripts, and instead continued along the path set for him by his family. After finishing Brienne, he put in a year at the new École Militaire in Paris, graduating in 1785. Opting for the relatively meritocratic artillery over the infantry, he received a first posting to the quiet Rhône River town of Valence, where he read obsessively in his room, and had his first flirtations with women. In the fall of 1786, his father having died the previous year, he returned home to Corsica to help take care of family affairs. As the French army had a large surplus of officers, he extended his leave without difficulty, and indeed spent over half of the next five years back home. He had grown into a thin, somewhat awkward, untidy young man of just under average height. (The legend of exceptionally short stature, eagerly disseminated by his enemies, comes from the fact that he stood just 5'2" according to pre-metric system French measures—but these were not the same as British measures. He was actually 5'4" or 5'5", just an inch or two below the period's average adult male height). The family soon came to recognize him, rather than his gentle older brother, as its real leader. Indeed, his younger brother Lucien soon grasped the intensity of Napoleon's drive, writing the following to Joseph in 1792: "I have always detected in Napoleon an ambition that is not altogether selfish, but which overcomes his love for the common good.... He seems inclined to be a tyrant, and I think that he would be one if he were king."

What made it possible for Napoleon to follow the path of overweening ambition outside the world of literature was, of course, the French Revolution. For more than three years after the Revolution began, however, he confined his ambitions to Corsica. He certainly enthused over the early successes of the French National Assembly, declaring in June 1789 that "in an instant everything has changed. From the depths of this nation, an electric spark has exploded." But he spent most of his time at home in Corsica, hoping that the political upheaval might open new possibilities for him there. In June 1789 he wrote an obsequious letter introducing himself to the revered Corsican leader Pasquale Paoli, then still in exile in England, and universally known by Corsicans as the "Babbù," or father. "I was born," he told Paoli, "as the fatherland was dying. Thirty thousand Frenchmen, vomited upon our coasts, drowning the seat of liberty in torrents of blood: this was the spectacle that first impressed itself upon my sight."

When the National Assembly voted an amnesty for Paoli a few months later, allowing him to return home, Napoleon rejoiced. The island soon found itself divided between a "French party" and Paoli's "Corsican party," and Napoleon sided eagerly with the latter. He joined political clubs, pushed Joseph to run for office (unsuccessfully), and then, in April 1792, himself won election to a lieutenant-colonelcy in the new revolutionary National Guard (a position he could hold while remaining a lieutenant in the French army). By the summer of 1792, as he later put it, he "no longer had that small ambition to become an author."

Yet Corsican politics soon turned out to be a morass that offered Napoleon little but frustration. In France itself, the Revolution was overturning age-old hierarchies and giving worldwide prominence to previously obscure figures like Maximilien Robespierre, a small-town lawyer, or Jean-Paul Marat, a mentally unstable Swiss doctor. But in Corsica the grip of the dominant clans—the Salicettis, the Pozzo di Borgos, the Buttafuocos—remained strong, making it hard for a distinctly second-tier Buonaparte to rise to their level. By the fall of 1792 Napoleon had also succeeded in seriously annoying the Babbù, who groused about the Buonaparte brothers, calling them "ragazzoni inesperti" (inexperienced boys).

Matters came to a head in the winter and spring of 1792–93—the period that in France itself saw the foundation of the Republic, the execution of King Louis XVI, and the beginnings of civil war. In February, Napoleon gained his first taste of combat in an expedition dispatched to conquer a neighboring Italian island that ended in a fiasco. Paoli had quite possibly sent him along in the hope the young officer might meet with a stray bullet. Paoli himself was moving toward a break with the rapidly radicalizing government in Paris, presenting the Buonaparte family with the stark choice between their increasingly inhospitable home island and an increasingly turbulent mainland. It was the hotheaded Lucien, the brother most favorable to the Revolution, who effectively settled matters in March 1793 by giving a speech to the radical Jacobin Club of Toulon, on the French Mediterranean coast, denouncing Paoli as a tyrant. The speech provided part of the justification when the National Convention in Paris ordered Paoli's arrest in April and then assembled a military expedition to reimpose French authority in Corsica. Napoleon himself took part in the expedition, while Paoli angrily denounced the Buonapartes as traitors. When it became clear, in June, that the French did not have sufficient strength to drive Paoli from Corsica, the family fled to the mainland. An angry Paolist crowd pillaged their home in Ajaccio.

Although these events dramatically dissolved Napoleon's ties to Corsica, they did not immediately bind his future to France. He knew that the currents of French revolutionary politics were exceptionally swift and treacherous, especially for a family which had enthusiastically claimed membership in the French nobility. Furthermore, in eighteenth-century Europe army officers frequently moved from one country to another in search of better professional opportunities, drawing the line only at fighting against their own homelands. We know that as late as 1795 Napoleon applied for a posting to the army of the Turkish sultan. One can only imagine how differently the history of Europe might have played out had he taken it up.

Nonetheless, the years 1793–95 did prove crucial for Napoleon. In the spring of 1793, not long after Lucien's speech in Toulon, the port city revolted against the revolutionary government and invited the British navy to use it as a base. Napoleon became part of the French army that besieged Toulon, and the campaign provided him with his first great chance to shine. He had a stroke of luck when the commander of the artillery was wounded and Christophe Salicetti, a Corsican member of the National Convention and patron of the Buonapartes, named him to the vacant position. Napoleon showed political ruthlessness immediately, denouncing superior officers to the dictatorial

Committee of Public Safety in order to get his own battle plans approved. He also demonstrated his tremendous energy and military acumen by effectively reorganizing the artillery, identifying a crucial weak point in Toulon's defenses and leading the attack against it personally. He demonstrated genuine physical courage as well, receiving a bayonet wound to the thigh and having a horse shot out from under him. Toulon fell to the Republic, and another powerful deputy wrote to Paris praising Napoleon as an officer of "transcendent merit." Still just twenty-four years old, he was promoted to the rank of brigadier general.

Yet the currents of revolutionary politics remained difficult to navigate. The deputy who had praised Napoleon was Augustin Robespierre, brother of Maximilien, and Napoleon now found himself bound to the radical Robespierrist faction, the architects of the Reign of Terror. Napoleon saw much to admire in Robespierre, who seemed committed to building up a powerful state apparatus and restoring social stability. But in July 1794 the Robespierrists fell from power. Augustin committed suicide; Maximilien died the next day on the guillotine, along with his principal followers. Napoleon, along with many other officers linked to the faction, was arrested and spent nearly two weeks confined to quarters. And while the new authorities decided not to prosecute him, during the next year he found himself assigned to staff positions, far from the combat posts where a host of other young generals were winning glory and rapid advancement. (The average age of new French generals in the 1790s was just thirty-three.) One memorandum he wrote at the time does give an excellent glimpse of the development of his strategic and political thought, stressing "the absolute necessity, in an immense fight like ours, for a revolutionary government and a single, central authority." But Napoleon's frustration again grew. In May 1795, he received the thankless assignment of helping to chase down the last remnants of counterrevolutionary guerrillas in western France. He delayed taking it up, and it was at this point that he put in for the Turkish commission, only to have the French government veto the request. A French official at the time described him as "a young man of pale and livid complexion, stooped, looking frail and sickly."

But once again, the combination of skill, energy, ruthlessness, and sheer luck that had served Napoleon so well at Toulon came to his rescue. In the summer of 1795, the National Convention approved a new constitution—France's third since the start of the Revolution—but undemocratically reserved two-thirds of the slots in the new legislature for members of the existing government. Conservatives hoping for a return to constitutional monarchy protested vehemently and in early October 1795 took to arms in the streets of Paris. Defense of the government fell to a dissolute former noble named Paul Barras, a member of the Convention who had helped lead the coup against the Robespierrists.

Earlier, as it happened, Barras had helped oversee the siege of Toulon. Now he called on the capable young officer who had done so much to defeat the rebels there. On the crucial day of October 5, the 13th of Vendémiaire by the new revolutionary calendar, Barras used the French army to crush the threatened royalist insurrection, leaving hundreds dead. According to legend, Napoleon placed cannon near the church of Saint-Roch on the rue Saint-Honoré in central Paris and ordered his men to give the insurgents a deadly "whiff of grapeshot." Most likely this particular incident never took place, but Napoleon's skill in organizing the defense and deploying troops and artillery in the narrow streets of central Paris did win him high praise from Barras. Within two weeks he had been given command of the Army of the Interior, one of the largest in France, with a high salary and lucrative appointments for his brothers Joseph and Lucien as well.

Soon enough, Barras brought one other crucial change to Napoleon's life, introducing him to a former mistress, Rose de Beauharnais. An aristocrat from France's Caribbean colony of

2. In 1796 Napoleon married the glamorous aristocratic widow Rose ("Josephine") de Beauharnais, seen here in a portrait by Pierre-Paul Prud'hon. She was empress of France from 1804 until the couple's divorce in 1810.

Martinique, Rose had lost her husband to the guillotine during the Terror and barely escaped with her own life. Now in her early thirties, with two adolescent children, Barras considered her used goods, but to Napoleon she seemed the epitome of seductive beauty. He might no longer aspire to write romantic fiction, but romantic fiction shaped his own reactions, and he fell hard. "Sweet and incomparable Joséphine, what a strange effect you have on my heart!" he wrote her two months after they had met. "I draw from your lips, from your heart, a flame that burns me.... I will see you in three hours. In the meantime, *mio dolce amor*, here are a thousand kisses; but give me none, for they burn my blood." Napoleon was not a complete romantic novice. During his time in southern France he had courted a silk merchant's daughter named Désirée Clary, who eventually married his fellow officer Jean-Baptiste Bernadotte. (By one of the Napoleonic period's stranger turns of fate, they ended up king and queen of Sweden, and their descendants still sit on Sweden's throne.) But with Rose, things were much more serious, and after six months he prevailed on the older woman to marry him, much to the displeasure of his own family. She thereafter went by the name he bestowed on her: Joséphine. Her ardor never matched his, and she took lovers when he left on campaign, causing him considerable anguish.

And he left almost immediately after their wedding in the spring of 1796, because his rise to political prominence had come at a perfectly opportune moment. In 1793–94, the new-born French Republic had fought its way back against a large European coalition, even as it brutally eliminated its remaining domestic rebels. Despite the chaos that accompanied the radical Revolution, the ability of the new regime to draw on the country's vast human and material resources eventually weighed heavily in the balance. As the great military writer Carl von Clausewitz later wrote, "in 1793 a force appeared that beggared all imagination. Suddenly war again became the business of the people—a people of thirty millions, all of whom considered themselves to be citizens.... Nothing now impeded the vigor with which war could be waged,

and consequently the opponents of France faced the utmost peril."
In 1795 France occupied the Netherlands, while Spain and
Prussia both withdrew from the conflict. Now the Republic could
go on an ambitious new offensive, and its strategists devised a
three-pronged attack to the east, aimed at defeating the major
remaining continental enemy, the Austrian Empire. One French
army would strike northeast from France into Rhineland
Germany. A second would advance east into southern Germany.
And a third, the Army of Italy, principally as a diversion to help
the other two, would attack northern Italy, much of it ruled by
Austria. Named to the command of this third, smallest army was
Napoleon Bonaparte, his dreams of Corsica now far behind him.

Chapter 2
The general, 1796–1799

More than twenty years after defeating the Austrian army at Lodi, Napoleon Bonaparte confided to the tiny retinue accompanying him in exile that only after that battle "did I believe myself to be a superior man, and did the ambition come to me of executing the great things which so far had been occupying my thoughts only as a fantastic dream." The words are easily dismissed as nostalgic bombast, but surely very few human beings have ever experienced what Napoleon did between mid-1796 and late 1799. At the start of this period, just twenty-six years old, he was already an important French general, but still just one of several. Three and a half years later, he was, without exaggeration, the new Caesar.

It was the French Revolution that made this stupefying ascent possible. The Revolution badly damaged the traditional hierarchies of French society, opening the door to radically new forms of social mobility and political power. It also unleashed newly intense forms of war, and provided French rulers with new ways to harness their country's formidable natural resources against its enemies. The different forms of change operated in tandem, war driving politics and politics driving war.

But history is not just a matter of impersonal forces, and nothing ensured that an individual would come along to exploit the changes as fully and spectacularly as Napoleon. Many are the historical opportunities that have been lost for lack of talent or vision, and many are the individuals who came into history at the wrong time and place to make the mark they could have. "Full many a gem of purest ray serene / The dark unfathomed caves of ocean bear," wrote the English poet Thomas Grey. But in Napoleon's case, for better or for worse (for millions, it would be for worse), the man met his hour. He showed that he not only had genius, but a genius perfectly suited to the circumstances of 1796.

The genius was of two sorts, military and political. The former was grounded in genuinely extraordinary mental abilities that he had now had the chance to display to the fullest. He had a nearly photographic memory and the ability to visualize the positions of thousands of men in scores of separate units, along with salient details about munitions and supplies. He could see in a moment how to maneuver everything for maximum effect. These skills perfectly suited the style of war the French army had been developing since well before 1789, which stressed mobility, including even of artillery. A classic Napoleonic tactic involved dividing his forces into a number of groups, ten miles or more distant from each other, followed by rapid forced marches to bring them together at a single strategic spot, coupled with enveloping moves to disrupt enemy operations. The goal was not simply to outmaneuver enemies, but to smash their armies entirely.

Napoleon's genius in this respect depended in turn on a ferocious stamina, which he also possessed in abundance—to quote Ralph Waldo Emerson, who wrote one of the most interesting nineteenth-century portraits of Napoleon, he was "a man of stone and iron." Napoleon was also one of the first army commanders to use a chief of staff—the talented Louis-Alexandre Berthier—to coordinate his orders. In 1796 and 1797 alone, with Berthier's help, Napoleon wrote or dictated nearly two thousand letters, on everything from the number of carts needed to carry a regiment's paperwork to the position of drummer-boys in a marching column. He required little sleep, routinely rising soon after midnight and working through to the next evening, with only a short morning nap to refresh himself. "What a pity he wasn't lazy," his foreign minister Talleyrand later quipped.

His political genius was just as important. Napoleon understood, far better than his rivals, and far better than his predecessors on the merry-go-round of French revolutionary politics, that in a newly democratic age, political success depended on forging a bond with ordinary people. And forging it involved a double strategy. On the one hand, for ordinary people to have a reason to follow and support him, they had to recognize his extraordinary qualities and even consider him a potential savior. But for them to feel the attachment passionately, to become ready to sacrifice for him, they also had to identify with him, to feel as if they knew him personally. To quote Emerson again: "The man in the street finds in [Napoleon] the qualities and powers of other men in the street." Napoleon had an instinctive flair for presenting himself as both savior and intimate acquaintance, and in every medium available to him: oratory, the visual arts, and above all, print.

Napoleon's soldiers did not immediately see this genius when he took over command of the Army of Italy. He still cut an unimpressive figure: "small, skinny, very pale, with big black eyes and sunken cheeks," in the words of one sergeant. But the general quickly went to work improving the soldiers' conditions, increasing their pay and ensuring that they received regular rations of meat, bread, and brandy. (A regular alcohol ration was a treasured privilege for early modern soldiers, who often went into battle drunk.) In his first proclamation to the army, Napoleon called the men his "brothers in arms." He allowed them to address him with the familiar "tu." Soon he had won not only their respect but that of his rivals, who had initially dismissed him as a "political general" fit only for Parisian intrigues. "That little bugger scares me," said Pierre Augereau, later one of his top commanders.

But it was Napoleon's opponents who had the most reason to be frightened. Within a month of taking command of the army, he led its thirty-six thousand men into Italy and engaged Austria's ally, the northern Italian state of Piedmont, in a series of fast-moving battles. Within two weeks he had driven the Piedmontese out of the war. He then confronted the main Austrian force. By his own telling, the battle of Lodi, on May 10, was not itself a major victory, for the Austrians were already in retreat. Nonetheless, the spectacular crossing of a bridge over the Adda River, with Napoleon personally overseeing operations on the front lines, capped a series of brilliant maneuvers and allowed the French to occupy northern Italy's major city, Milan, a few days later. A campaign originally planned as a diversion from the main French operations further north had now become, by virtue of success, the focal point of French efforts.

It would take another nine months and an exhausting string of battles for Napoleon to consolidate these early victories. But in most of the battles, the Austrians lost far more men than the French and failed in their attempts to relieve their great strategic strongpoint in northern Italy, the citadel of Mantua. Finally, on January 14–15, 1797, near the small town of Rivoli, Napoleon's army confronted that of Austrian general Josef Alvinczy, who was making one last great push toward Mantua. It was a classic Napoleonic battle. The night before, Napoleon rode up to the heights overlooking the field, lit brilliantly by moonlight, to observe the enemy positions. The battle itself depended on the quick redeployment of his forces. At one crucial moment, Austrian grenadiers charged into a central gorge near the Adige River, and Napoleon pulled back several of his brigades to meet them, having calculated that the Austrians elsewhere were too exhausted to take advantage of the maneuver and move into the gap. A French charge then sent the grenadiers running, upon which Napoleon rushed his men back to their earlier positions, from where they succeeded in splitting Alvinczy's army in two. The result was the virtual destruction of the Austrians, who lost fourteen thousand

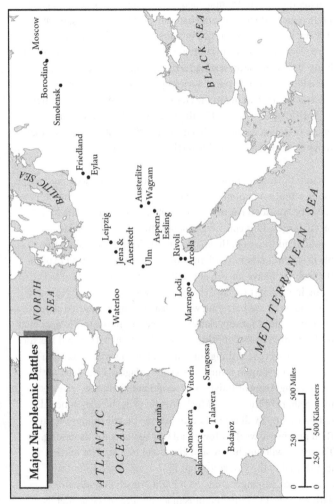

3. Major Napoleonic battles.

men to Napoleon's five thousand. And with the last chance for its relief squandered, Mantua finally surrendered two weeks later, leaving the road to Vienna open. The battle only confirmed what French general Henri Clarke had reported back to the government in Paris about Napoleon two months before: "There is no one here who does not regard him as a genius." Meanwhile, Napoleon himself turned south, seizing territory from the states ruled by Pope Pius VI. At this point, serious peace negotiations with Austria began, leading to the signing of a preliminary agreement in April 1797 at Leoben. The final treaty confirmed not only France's Italian gains but also its annexation both of present-day Belgium and of considerable territory in Germany.

Even in the midst of these intense operations, Napoleon paid as much attention to politics as to military matters, engaging in what could be considered a two-pronged political offensive. Its first prong targeted his core constituency: his own soldiers. He made frequent addresses to them, praising their bravery, calling them his brothers, and even insisting, on one occasion, "I can't express the feelings I have for you any better than by saying that I bear along in my heart the love that you show me every day." He doled out medals by the barrelful, while distributing a hundred specially engraved sabers for especially valiant acts of heroism. He appealed to the soldiers' sense of pride and destiny: "The fatherland has the right to expect great things of you . . . All of you wish to be able to say with pride, upon returning to your villages, 'I was part of the conquering Army of Italy!' "And he did not hesitate to give his men a share of the spoils. Much later, in exile, he remembered telling them: "I will lead you into the most fertile plains on earth. Rich provinces, wealthy towns, all will be yours for the taking. There you will find honor, and glory, and riches." The soldiers in fact shared in the vast sums that France extracted from Italy during the campaign: some 45 million French pounds, along with another 12 million pounds in jewels and precious metals, and more than three hundred priceless paintings and sculptures. (Napoleon, building on French revolutionary precedents, was determined to make "war pay for war" and not to rely on Paris for funds.) Napoleon also took care to remain personally approachable. At the Battle of Lodi, this former artillery officer allegedly stepped in to help load cannon at a critical moment, and made sure that the tale circulated through the ranks. He did nothing to dissuade the men from calling him by a nickname his aristocratic predecessors would have loathed: "the little corporal."

The second prong, meanwhile, was aimed squarely at the French public. Napoleon ensured that everyone back home knew of his exploits and appreciated his brilliance. During the campaign, artists made no fewer than thirty-seven portraits of him, many of which he commissioned directly. The great painter Antoine-Jean Gros brilliantly captured a moment of heroism from the Battle of Arcola in November 1796: Napoleon, flag in hand, leading his men over a bridge under heavy Austrian fire (see the cover of this book). The facts that the attack had failed and that Napoleon's subordinate Augereau displayed even more bravery were tactfully ignored. Napoleon founded two French-language newspapers to report on his conquests—one aimed at radical "neo-Jacobins," the second at a more moderate audience. In October 1797 the first of them celebrated him as a virtual demigod:

> Today, glory has written a new name on its immortal tablets, with no fear of it ever being erased. The divinations that predicted a brilliant destiny for the young islander have come true. The time is past in which he locked himself up in his tent, a voluntary prisoner, a new Archimedes always at work.... He promised victory, and brought it. He flies like lightning, and strikes like thunder. The speed of his movements is matched only by their accuracy and prudence. He is everywhere. He sees everything. Like a comet cleaving the clouds, he appears at the same moment on the astonished banks of two separate rivers.

Today, it is hard to take prose like this seriously. But the French public, which had previously deified writers like Jean-Jacques

Rousseau and had even, briefly, heaped similar accolades on the shoulders of King Louis XVI (before he tried to flee the country and join a counterrevolutionary army), had a ready appetite for over-the-top hero worship. It helped, of course, that under the hype and exaggeration lay Napoleon's truly impressive achievements. So writers in France soon reinforced Napoleon's legend on their own, with poets publishing odes to his glory, playwrights composing at least a dozen plays and one opera about the Italian campaign, biographers inventing childhood exploits for him, and journalists founding a newspaper titled *Journal of Bonaparte and Virtuous Men*.

Whether or not Napoleon was already dreaming of taking power, this nascent cult of personality allowed him to carve out a remarkably independent political role. In France, Barras and the other politicians he had helped keep in power in 1795 had created a new regime with limited suffrage, governed by a five-man executive Directory. Already in the spring of 1796, Napoleon felt sufficiently confident simply to ignore orders from the Directory if he disagreed with them. In the fall, it was he, more than the Directors, who took the initiative in grouping several Italian states together into a new political federation. After Napoleon's triumph at Rivoli, instructions from Paris turned positively deferential: "The Directory wishes you to understand that it is not giving you an order, but merely formulating a request…" "When voters in the new Italian federation rejected French-approved candidates, Napoleon simply dissolved it. Then, largely on his own initiative, he brought together all his conquered Italian territories into a subservient "Cisalpine Republic," which he personally inaugurated with overblown pomp in its new capital city, Milan. It is worth remembering, though, that a great many Italians welcomed their freedom from their former rulers and approved of the principles of the French Revolution. Despite the large sums looted from Italy by the French, these "Giaccobini" cheered Napoleon as a Liberator.

Not all Italians shared their enthusiasm, however, and in dealing with rebels and insurgents Napoleon revealed another important side of his personality: absolute ruthlessness. Soon after his initial victories, the city of Pavia rose up in revolt against the French, supported by several thousand peasants, mostly armed with hunting weapons and pitchforks. A French mobile column intercepted one peasant group near the town of Binasco, killed a hundred of them, put the rest to flight, and then burned the town while shooting all the adult men they could find. After Pavia itself surrendered, Napoleon let his troops run wild there for a day, raping and looting. Other Italian towns soon suffered much the same fate. Such behavior was standard operating practice in eighteenth-century European warfare (despite the overall decline in atrocities from earlier centuries). Indeed, in the Revolution, parts of France had seen much worse. For the moment, at least, the repression also kept northern and central Italy firmly in France's orbit. But it made the image of the "revolutionary liberator" rather less convincing.

A similar tension between pragmatism and revolutionary principle ran through Napoleon's diplomacy, as the Italian campaign came to its conclusion. When France and Austria signed the Treaty of Campo Formio in October 1797, the preamble listed four Austrian "plenipotentiaries," each with long, ornate titles: in one case, "Marquis of Gallo, peer of Naples, Knight of the Royal Order of Saint Januarius, gentleman-of-the-bed-chamber of His Majesty the King of the Two Sicilies, and his Ambassador Extraordinary." The text then noted, rather more tersely: "The French Republic has appointed [as plenipotentiary] Bonaparte, general-in-chief of the French army in Italy." Such was the style of a democratic republic. But the same treaty summarily put an end to the centuries-old, independent Republic of Venice and without the slightest concern for the will of its people transferred them to Austrian sovereignty, to compensate Austria for its losses elsewhere. Napoleon himself had spent the previous summer at the sumptuous Italian château of Mombello, where he insisted on punctilious courtly etiquette, even dining in front of an audience in the manner of France's King Louis XIV. When he arrived for the Congress of Rastatt in December to discuss further territorial adjustments in Germany, he did so in a magnificent carriage pulled by eight horses—an appurtenance traditionally reserved for crowned sovereigns.

To the French themselves, though, he continued to pose as a revolutionary. In the summer of 1797, conservatives hoping to restore a constitutional monarchy had made surprising headway in French elections. Desperate to stop them, the so-called neo-Jacobins looked for support from the armies, which still bore the imprint of the radical revolution and were still fighting against Old Regime sovereigns. Neo-Jacobin journalists painted the conservatives as corrupt conspirators and Paris as an Augean Stables in need of a military broom. "The great deluge was necessary to purge the earth," one of them wrote. "We need the armies to purify France." Napoleon and several other commanders gave their assent and dispatched troops to the capital. In September 1797 a coup took place in which the neo-Jacobins purged their rivals from the Directory and the assemblies. It was the first time the armed forces had intervened directly to change a French regime, and it set an ominous precedent. It also led to the removal of civilian commissioners from the army, giving Napoleon and other generals even more autonomy than before.

But whatever Napoleon's true political beliefs were at this point, already by the end of 1797, at age twenty-eight, he had become one of the most powerful men on the continent: in Italy a prince deciding the fate of states; in France a savior of the Republic. His greatest anxiety did not concern the war, which had now ended on the continent and continued only on the high seas against Great Britain. It focused rather on Joséphine, with whom he remained besotted but who clearly was not so besotted with him, despite his triumphs. During the Italian campaign she had mostly remained in Paris, often failed to answer his letters, and for a time taken a handsome young cavalry officer as a lover. His letters to her lurched wildly between theatrical despair and theatrical anger.

"Your letters are cold like middle age; they resemble fifteen years of marriage," he moaned in October 1796. "Fie, Joséphine! It is so mean, so bad, so treasonous of you." A month later he was threatening death: "I hate you.... Beware, Joséphine! One fine night the doors will be smashed in and there I will be in your bed. Remember! Othello's little dagger!" When he returned to Paris in December 1797, the breach was far from healed.

He also had difficult decisions to make about his career. Where should he go, with France now largely at peace? His popularity was immense—thousands attended a public festival in his honor—and he was already imagining himself as the country's supreme leader. His secretary later remembered him saying: "I ought to overthrow them, and make myself King." He explored the possibility of becoming a member of the Directory but found it would require a constitutional change to the minimum age, then set at forty. He was named to command of the new Army of England and charged with preparing an invasion across the Channel, but he quickly realized that France simply did not have sufficient naval strength for the purpose when set against Britain's formidable Royal Navy. Instead he ended up taking a very different direction, thanks in part to a man whose story now became inextricably entwined with his own.

Charles-Maurice de Talleyrand made an odd match for Napoleon. The young general personified boldness, ambition, physical energy and overblown operatic passion; the sickly, clubfooted Talleyrand was a creature of subtlety, irony, and world-weary cynicism. Fifteen years Napoleon's senior, he had been born into one of France's great noble families and, with his physical infirmities ruling out a military career, had gone into the Church. At just thirty-four he was named a bishop. Then, in 1789, he became a liberal revolutionary but fled the country when the monarchy fell, washing up in Pennsylvania, where he briefly dabbled in backwoods land speculation. Soon after returning to France after the end of the Terror, he was appointed foreign minister and argued

that for the sake of the country's economic health, France needed
to rebuild its once vast colonial empire. The Seven Years' War of
1756–63 against Britain had reduced the empire to a scattering
of Atlantic and Indian Ocean islands and Saint-Domingue
(Haiti), and in 1797 France was fast losing the latter to black
revolutionaries. On this issue, Talleyrand's interests and
Napoleon's coincided perfectly.

At various points in the eighteenth century, France had cast a
covetous glance toward Egypt as a possible site of colonization.
Ruled by the warrior caste of the Mamelukes under the nominal
aegis of the Turks' Ottoman Empire, the country possessed a
strategic position on both the Mediterranean and Red Seas.
(In theory, it could even serve as a base for attacking Britain's
colonies in India.) For Napoleon, the idea of conquering it served
a triple purpose. It gave him the perfect excuse to withdraw
from a political scene that was not yet ready for him. It offered
him the chance to add even more laurels to his reputation—and
what better destination, for a man so frequently compared to
Alexander the Great and Caesar, than a country both had
conquered in their days?

Finally, somewhat counterintuitively, it allowed him to burnish his
reputation as the most "civilian" of French generals. As Napoleon
knew very well, comparisons to Julius Caesar were mostly not a
compliment in revolutionary France. As early as 1789, warnings
had sounded in the press and assemblies about overpowerful
generals taking power, and the 1797 coup Napoleon had abetted
did nothing to mute the chorus. "Is the Rubicon already crossed?"
asked one right-wing newspaper in its aftermath, referring to the
original Caesar's decisive step toward dictatorship. "Will we
manage to avoid a military republic?" On returning to France,
to assuage these fears, Napoleon ostentatiously adopted civilian
clothing and became a member of the elite National Institute, the
successor to the learned scientific and literary academies of the
Old Regime. When he began to promote the idea of an Egyptian

campaign, he spoke of how it could promote the interests of French scientists and scholars and proposed turning the supposedly corrupt, "oriental" Egypt into a model of enlightened administration.

Since it also served the purposes of the Directory to put this popular and ambitious general at a far remove (1,690 miles) from France, they quickly approved the plan. In May 1798, one of the largest French naval expeditions in memory set out from the port of Toulon, stopped en route to conquer Malta, dodged the British navy, and on July 1 appeared off the sweltering, sun-baked coast of Alexandria. The next day, some four thousand French soldiers scaled the walls of the ancient city and compelled its surrender. A week after that, having landed and organized his army, Napoleon began a 120-mile march toward Egypt's capital, Cairo.

The march again showed just how effective a leader Napoleon could be. It took place under North Africa's blasting midsummer sun; the soldiers wore heavy cloth uniforms and carried sixty to eighty pounds of equipment and supplies on their backs. "We saw them die of thirst, of starvation, of heat," one staff officer later wrote to his parents. "Others, seeing how their comrades were suffering, blew their brains out; some threw themselves into the Nile." The soldiers had no bread and subsisted on a diet of pumpkins, melons, and chickens. Yet Napoleon himself shared these discomforts, sometimes himself going a whole day without food, and he constantly urged the men on with the promise of rich spoils and glory. Despite the harsh conditions, the army arrived outside of Cairo in good condition and on July 21 fought the main Mameluke force in the Battle of the Pyramids, within sight of these most famous Egyptian monuments. The French were well-trained and well-equipped and possessed deadly mobile artillery that the Mamelukes could not match. When the Mamelukes tried to make use of their legendary cavalry, the French formed impregnable infantry squares from which they fired devastating musket salvos. Before the battle, Napoleon made one of his most well-known speeches to his assembled men: "Soldiers, do your duty. Consider that from the top of these monuments forty centuries are looking down upon you." By the end of the battle the pyramids, and Egypt itself, were in his hands.

In Italy, Napoleon had found his freedom of action limited by his instructions from Paris, at least in part, and by the need to respect, at least in theory, the Italians' democratic aspirations. In Egypt he could rule without interference. He put a new government in place, based on a system of native councils. There would be a new Egyptian court system, a postal service, hospitals, and a National Guard. He would introduce land reform. He did not want to make the country into a democracy. This new, enlightened Egypt would be based on civic equality and the rational management of social interests by "enlightened" colonial rulers, but not on liberty and self-determination. (The native councils routinely found themselves overruled by the French authorities.) Meanwhile, in keeping with the "civilian" profile he had tried so hard to establish back in Paris, Napoleon poured much of his enthusiasm into a learned institute, on the French model, that he staffed with 160 scholars, artists, and engineers who had come with him from France. The members met twice a week to discuss everything from the wings of Egyptian ostriches to the composition of the slime of the Nile and Egyptian antiquities. They generally had little respect for the native Egyptians, whom they perceived as stereotypically backward and lazy "orientals" living amid the ruins of ancient glory. Yet their efforts did pay dividends, bringing much new information about the country to European eyes through the massive *Description of Egypt*, which was published starting in 1809, and through the discovery of the Rosetta Stone, which ultimately permitted the deciphering of Egyptian hieroglyphics.

Napoleon himself was utterly entranced with Egypt. Here he was, still not yet thirty years old, standing in triumph where Alexander and Caesar had stood before him, surrounded by an exotic and seemingly submissive people. The experience fed the romantic streak in his character that his early reading had kindled and that had previously expressed itself mostly in his fixation on Josephine. Now he took the first in a series of mistresses and indulged fantasies of carving out a new empire in the East. His propagandists—as in Italy, he sedulously cultivated his image—egged him on. A piece of Arabic verse published in one of the new Egyptian newspapers he founded read: "Kings bow their proud heads before the invincible BONAPARTE, the lion of battles…the heavens of glory bow down before him." It helped that, unlike earlier European invaders of the Middle East, this veteran of the radical French Revolution had little remaining attachment to Christianity.

Indeed, he hinted that he might even abandon it for Islam. "We Frenchmen," he wrote to the pasha of Aleppo, "are no longer the infidels who…came to fight against your faith; we realize how sublime it is; *we profess it ourselves*; and the moment has come for all Frenchmen to…become believers like yourselves." He took to reading the Koran and engaged in discussions with Muslim clerics. "In Egypt," he later mused, "I found myself freed from the obstacles of an irksome civilization. I was full of dreams. I saw myself founding a religion, marching into Asia, riding an elephant, a turban on my head and in my hand a new Koran that I would have composed to suit my need." The time he spent in the country, he added, "was the most beautiful of my life because it was most ideal." For the many years afterward he would surround himself with mementos of Egypt, including a living one: a Mameluke bodyguard.

Yet if the fantasy was rich, reality soon conspired to undermine it. Just a month after the French had arrived, Admiral Horatio Nelson decimated the French fleet in the Battle of Aboukir Bay, cutting Napoleon off from France and dooming any chance that France might establish naval parity with Britain. The Egyptians themselves, meanwhile, refused to play the submissive role he had assigned them, and in October the city of Cairo staged a revolt.

After brutally repressing it, with a death toll in the thousands, Napoleon displayed the same ruthlessness as in Italy, coldly ordering his men to behead three hundred more rebels and throw their corpses into the Nile. Meanwhile, the invasion helped provoke the formation of a new, broad-based coalition against France, and the start of a new period of large-scale European war. Austria returned to the fight, joining Britain, and two new allies—Russia, and of course Ottoman Turkey, whose territory Napoleon had invaded.

It was precisely to take preemptive action against the Turks that, in February 1799, Napoleon decided to invade the neighboring Ottoman province of Syria. With thirteen thousand troops, he marched east from Egypt and up the coast of Palestine. On March 7 they took Jaffa, near present-day Tel Aviv, and here Napoleon gave an example of ruthlessness and cruelty that went well beyond the customary practices of the day. In order to intimidate the population and impress the Turkish commanders, he gave his troops free rein to sack and pillage for days after Jaffa had surrendered. He also ordered three thousand captured enemy soldiers taken down to the beach and shot, claiming he did not have the manpower to hold them prisoner. This last decision spurred an anguished discussion among his generals, which Napoleon supposedly ended by screaming at his closest aide, Berthier, that if he felt squeamish, he could go off and become a monk. "Sooner or later," a soldier wrote home, "the blood of these 3,000 victims will be upon us."

The Egyptian colony's future was already dire, thanks to Lord Nelson, but now the situation started to deteriorate rapidly. Napoleon continued up the Palestinian coast, but nearly three thousand of his men fell ill with plague, while British marines captured much of his artillery. Near present-day Haifa, Napoleon personally led several frantic attacks on the walled citadel of Acre, but with the British supplying the defenders from the sea, it held out. Napoleon and General Jean-Baptiste Kléber did manage to defeat a much larger Turkish army at Mount Tabor, near Nazareth, but the Syrian campaign still ended in failure, and the French retreated to Egypt. In July, the British landed a Turkish army near Alexandria, but Napoleon decisively defeated them, thanks above all to a brilliantly executed cavalry charge by General Joachim Murat, the son of an innkeeper, who next year would marry Napoleon's younger sister, Caroline. But given British control of the Mediterranean, even this victory could only stave off the inevitable.

Napoleon had little desire to preside personally over the colony's demise, and at the same time he realized that France itself was now ready for his return. Two more coups d'état had taken place there since 1797, with the Directory lurching violently between left and right. Civil unrest had intensified, and the regime had given the army the right to place large areas of the country under effective martial law. The new dominant figure of the Directory, a former church official and hero of the early Revolution named Emmanuel-Joseph Sieyès, made it clear that he wanted "a sword"—a general—to help restore political stability. Meanwhile, rebellions were breaking out throughout French-dominated Italy, and the new alliance against revolutionary France—the so-called Second Coalition—was driving the Republic's armies back across Europe. By the summer of 1799, most of Napoleon's Italian gains had been reversed, and France itself seemed threatened with invasion, forcing the Directory to adopt a new version of the "war Jacobinism" that had helped save the Republic five years earlier. In one move that would have lasting importance for Napoleon, the Republic adopted a new, regular system of conscription that in theory made all men between the ages of twenty and twenty-five eligible for military service. By early fall, the reinforced French armies had ended the invasion threat, but the overall military situation still looked tenuous.

It was precisely at this moment that Napoleon and his top commanders embarked on two frigates, and, slipping past the

British Royal Navy, headed back to France, arriving in October. His successors in Egypt would hold onto the colony for another two years, but finally would surrender to the Turks and the British. Yet in 1799, as far as the French public knew, Egypt was still a brilliant success, and as Napoleon made his way north to Paris (where he would confront and then reconcile with Josephine), crowds cheered him enthusiastically. The city of Lyons even marked his arrival with a stage play entitled *The Return of the Hero*. Emmanuel Sieyès had tentatively approached other generals, but none of them enjoyed anything close to Napoleon's reputation, and Sieyès and Napoleon also had a shared belief in a well-ordered, rational political administration that privileged equality over liberty. Now, with Napoleon back, the two men met and agreed on plans to seize power. Talleyrand, who had resigned from the foreign ministry, also came into the conspiracy. The plot involved having allies among the elected deputies—including Napoleon's younger brother Lucien, now president of the lower house—push to adjourn the parliament to the suburban town of Saint-Cloud, under the watchful eyes of the army. There it would vote to replace the regime with three temporary executive "consuls": Napoleon, Sieyès himself, and another member of the Directory named Roger Ducos.

The coup itself, organized in haste, in fact came close to dissolving into failure and farce. On November 9—the Eighteenth Brumaire by the new revolutionary calendar—the parliament duly agreed to leave Paris. In an address to his soldiers, Napoleon excoriated the politicians for the recent military defeats. But the next day, in Saint-Cloud, a large number of deputies, wearing preposterous official uniforms of red togas and plumed hats, balked at the idea of handing over the last vestiges of democratic liberty. When Napoleon, more used to haranguing soldiers than to persuading civilian politicians, appeared before them in person, he grew unusually tongue-tied. "Don't forget," he stammered, "I walk with the God of war and the God of victory!" Loud protests burst out, and he fled the meeting hall.

Lucien Bonaparte saved the day. Outside the meeting hall, he addressed assembled soldiers and promised, theatrically brandishing a dagger, that he would commit fratricide if Napoleon ever became a tyrant. Thus encouraged, the soldiers escorted most of the deputies from the hall. Napoleon's future brother-in-law Joachim Murat supposedly shouted: "Citizens! You are dissolved!" The small number of trusted allies who remained then implemented the original plan, voting the Directory (and themselves) out of institutional existence and appointing the three consuls. These three men then oversaw the drafting of yet another constitution for the battered Republic.

To most of the population, it was not immediately obvious that very much had changed. The coup of the Eighteenth Brumaire was the fourth in little more than two years, and its most visible effect was to replace five Directors with three Consuls. Yet no single political figure in France since the start of the Revolution had possessed anything like Napoleon's personal appeal and charisma. "Our revolution," as his brother Lucien put it pompously but correctly in an anonymous pamphlet soon after the coup, "has given birth to greater events than it managed to give rise to men to contain them." Robespierre and the radical Jacobins had mostly been men of windy abstraction. Even the great orators Mirabeau and Danton did not attract anything like the adulation heaped on Napoleon. Napoleon was something new, and the keenest observers understood it. What did the new constitution mean, a woman was reportedly asked, at a public reading of the document? Her reply: "It means Bonaparte."

Chapter 3
The First Consul, 1799–1804

The French today do not much admire Napoleon Bonaparte, but to the extent they do, it is for his domestic achievements during the period 1799–1804, known as the Consulate. It was a period of authoritarian rule but also of energetic state-building, during which Napoleon established institutions and principles by which the French still govern themselves today. He himself described his purpose memorably in an address to one of these institutions, the Council of State, on May 8, 1802: "There is a government, but what is the rest of the nation? Grains of sand. . . . We have not established the Republic, and will not have done so, unless we manage to set down some masses of granite on the soil of France." Much of the granite set down between 1799 and 1804 still remains in place more than two centuries later. It is an open question whether it has truly benefited France or instead helped create what Alexis de Tocqueville, with Napoleon very much in mind, called "soft despotism": "an immense tutelary power, which assumes sole responsibility for securing [men's] pleasure and watching over their fate."

The achievement was nonetheless remarkable, given Napoleon's youth, and the fact that his principal executive experience had come from setting up satellite and colonial regimes in conquered territory while simultaneously directing major military operations. Yet he had a great deal working in his favor. By the fall of 1799, the

French had lived through a solid decade of revolutionary turmoil: large-scale internecine violence with a total death toll of more than three hundred thousand; a change of regime nearly every year; repeated bouts of hyperinflation and near economic collapse; threats of foreign invasion. Especially for people with property, security and order had become by far the leading political priorities. The Directory had already gone a long way toward transforming France into a "security state," but it had not brought political stability. Napoleon now promised to do so.

He also had a political vision that suited this moment of exhaustion. Despite his "Egyptian dreams," he was at this stage of his career an intensely practical man. He had little patience for the utopian visions of the radical revolutionaries, who had believed they could remake human nature itself. He mistrusted the very notion of political liberty, which in his view produced the kind of wild, dangerous political lurches that threatened the country's very survival. He considered himself a man of the Revolution, but what he admired in the Revolution was its hostility to undeserved social privilege, to intolerance and superstition, and to sloth and inefficiency disguised as tradition. He valued the Revolution's commitment to the rule of reason and to forms of civic equality that would allow men of talent to raise themselves in society. And like all but the most radical revolutionaries, he believed firmly in the importance of property and social stability. His brother Lucien, in his anonymous pamphlet supporting the new regime, praised "the class that property, learning, duty or interest call most insistently to the defense of the common weal" and claimed that Napoleon had rallied this class "against a deranged multitude."

Napoleon could also call on a talented cadre of men who shared and deepened his vision. Near the top of the government was, most important, Jean-Jacques Cambacérès, a portly ex-Jacobin lawyer from Montpellier capable of spending hundreds of thousands of francs a year on his principal passions: food and wine. After Napoleon's new constitution came into effect,

4. Europe in 1800.

Cambacérès took on the important, if subservient, role of Second
Consul to Napoleon's First, and oversaw most of the period's
domestic reforms. Further from the seat of power but still
important were a group of revolutionary intellectuals called the
"Ideologues"—they in fact invented the word, along with
"ideology," which they defined as the "science of ideas." They
believed that a proper understanding of how the mind worked
would allow them to instill rational beliefs and cooperative

48

behavior in the general population, thereby eliminating political strife, and perhaps even the need for political competition. They had helped found the learned Institute that Napoleon had eagerly joined a few years before. John Adams, among others, mocked their program, writing about "ideology": "What does it mean?… Does it mean Idiotism? The Science of Non compos Menticism? The Science of Lunacy?" But Napoleon took the concept seriously and made the leading Ideologue, Antoine Destutt de Tracy, a member of his elite Senate.

Napoleon could not hope to translate his ideas into granite-like institutions and practices, however, without first securing France against its foreign enemies and himself against his domestic ones. These were the preconditions for the Consulate's success, and in 1800 Napoleon set out to achieve them. The Second Coalition against France had already begun to crumble. Russia had withdrawn from the war in 1799. But Britain and Austria remained enemies of France, which had lost most of the Italian territories Napoleon had conquered three years before. And in the first few months of 1800, Napoleon's generals in the field lost even more ground. In early June, the last remaining French satellite state in Italy, the Ligurian Republic of Genoa, surrendered to Austria. In the political salons of Paris, gossips whispered that Napoleon had already lost his touch and might soon prove another victim of the wildly spinning carousel of French politics.

Rather than wait for subordinate generals to turn the situation around, Napoleon took a colossal gamble. In the spring, he put together an army of thirty-five thousand men from reserve forces in France and led them in person over one of the highest and most treacherous passes in the Alps, coming out into the north Italian plain, cutting off the Austrian army from its base and supplies. It was a spectacular coup, but the Austrians then rushed to meet him more quickly than he expected, and on June 14 the two armies clashed near the town of Marengo. The battle was a desperate one, in which French soldiers fired their muskets so often that they had to use their own urine to cool the barrels, to keep them from exploding when loaded with gunpowder. Napoleon, with his forces dangerously dispersed, came close to defeat, but he was saved when a dashing deputy, Louis Desaix, led back six thousand troops in time to hold off the main Austrian attack. The First Consul faced disaster again almost immediately when Desaix was shot and killed, but a decisive French cavalry charge finally broke apart the principal Austrian column. Even then, the Austrians might have dragged the French into a lengthy standoff, but their cautious commander lost heart and signed an armistice in which he agreed to pull out of Genoa and Lombardy. On July 2, Napoleon returned to Paris in triumph.

A general peace was now finally within reach. A few months after Marengo, General Jean-Victor Moreau scored another victory in Germany, bringing the war with Austria to a triumphant conclusion. (A peace was signed in early 1801.) Soon afterward, the viscerally anti-French William Pitt the Younger resigned as British prime minister, and his successor entered into talks with Napoleon as well, eventually signing a treaty at Amiens in the spring of 1802. Between 1800 and 1803 Napoleon also negotiated diplomatic agreements with the United States, Spain, Naples, Bavaria, Portugal, Russia, and the Ottoman Empire. France was now apparently secure—and, more important, secure within larger borders than it had ever known. The French Republic in 1802 included not just all of present-day France but Belgium as well, plus a large chunk of present-day Germany (the left bank of the Rhine River) and smaller pieces of Italy and the Netherlands. The Netherlands itself and northern Italy again took on the role of French satellite states.

Napoleon, with his instinct and genius for propaganda, exploited these achievements for everything they were worth. His hallelujah choir of poets, songwriters, painters, and sculptors took the credit for Marengo away from those who deserved it most—Desaix, the cavalry commander François Étienne de Kellermann, and Lady Luck—and heaped it on Napoleon's shoulders. They particularly hailed his daring crossing of the Saint Bernard pass, comparing it to Hannibal's similar feat two millennia previously. Napoleon had made the crossing wrapped in furs and riding a donkey, but the preeminent French artist of the day, Jacques-Louis David, painted him in a dashing red cape atop a magnificent rearing white charger in the single greatest and most memorable image of Napoleon ever executed. The propaganda worked. Marengo confirmed Napoleon's rise to power. It also, however, bound his

5. The painter Jacques-Louis David produced this unforgettable image of Napoleon crossing the Alps to invade Italy in 1800. In reality, Napoleon made the crossing wrapped in a blanket and riding a donkey.

power to military victory—he had effectively made a promise to the French people always to be victorious.

Domestic enemies proved just as dangerous as the Austrians. The surviving Jacobins in France saw the parallels between Bonaparte and Caesar all too clearly and rightly foresaw the end of the Republic if Napoleon were to consolidate his power. Conservatives, meanwhile, hoped that Napoleon might bring back

the exiled Bourbon pretender, Louis XVIII (brother of the
executed Louis XVI, whose son, also named Louis, had died
in a revolutionary prison) as king. They reacted angrily when
Napoleon failed to do so. Conspiracies formed on both sides; the
royalists were actively abetted by British agents. On Christmas
Eve 1800, Napoleon and Joséphine had a particularly close shave
when royalist terrorists loaded a cart with gunpowder and blew
it up as the First Consul's carriage passed by on the way to the
Opera—a "cart bomb," so to speak. At least eight people died,
including, allegedly, a small girl the terrorists had paid to hold the
cart's horse. But Napoleon survived unscathed and received wild
ovations when he appeared at the Opera a few minutes later. The
conspiracies in fact mostly backfired, for they gave Napoleon all
the more excuse to proceed with policies of naked political
repression, including close monitoring of private mail.

Napoleon soon made clear he would brook no serious domestic
opposition, and his chief agent in this regard was yet another of
the remarkable characters with whom he surrounded himself.
Joseph Fouché, the son of a naval officer, had originally embarked
on a career as a teacher in a Catholic religious order. In the
Revolution he quickly gravitated to the ultra-left, took part in
the bloody suppression of Lyons during the Terror, and made a
particular reputation among the "dechristianizers" of 1793–94,
erecting signs in Christian cemeteries reading "Death is an Eternal
Sleep." After becoming minister of police under the Directory, in
the summer of 1799 he joined in plotting the coup of the
Eighteenth Brumaire. Napoleon rewarded him with broad
powers, which Fouché used to set up an unprecedentedly
extended network of police spies and informers. In Paris, where
nearly the entire population lived in apartment buildings, Fouché
enlisted concierges as particularly valuable informers while his
men closely monitored the mail. He also introduced press
censorship of a sort France had not seen since the Old Regime.
Hundreds of newspapers had sprouted up in France during the
Revolution, but Napoleon and Fouché reduced the number to just

thirteen, eight of them in Paris, with a combined circulation of just twenty thousand (although each copy had several readers). Every page was cleared by censors before publication. After the Christmas Eve bombing, Napoleon suspected neo-Jacobins and ordered Fouché to begin a large-scale roundup. Fouché soon learned that the bombers had been royalists, but the crackdown on the left proceeded nonetheless.

Napoleon's authoritarianism manifested itself not only in this naked repression of political enemies but in the political system he created. Soon after the coup of the Eighteenth Brumaire, he shouldered aside Emmanuel Sieyès, and the new constitution stipulated that only one Consul, chosen for a term of ten years, would exercise real power. This constitution did provide for a parliament but restricted its powers by splitting it into the Tribunate, which had the right to discuss legislation but not vote, and the Legislative Assembly, which could vote but not discuss. The constitution gave all adult males voting rights, but a complex electoral system allowed the government to keep opponents off the lists of eligible representatives. An unelected Senate, whose members served for life, had the right to pronounce on the constitutionality of laws. Real power remained almost entirely vested in the executive, that is, Bonaparte. Unlike every previous revolutionary constitution, this one significantly lacked a declaration of rights. It was, however, a perfect expression of Napoleon's political vision. On its completion, he took the step of submitting it to a popular plebiscite. Out of 5.5 million eligible adult male voters, 1.5 million participated, and an overwhelming majority voted yes. The new minister of the interior—Lucien Bonaparte—inflated the yes total to 3 million so as to give the appearance of true majority support.

Two years later, with France at peace for the first time in a decade and the opposition largely cowed, Napoleon moved to solidify his position yet further. Over mild and hesitant opposition from his tame Senate, he insisted on yet another new constitution (the fifth in eleven years), which transformed him into Consul for Life and gave him the ability to choose his successor, while leaving most other aspects of the government as they were. Another plebiscite took place and delivered a large majority in favor, which the Interior Ministry again rigged to look even more impressive. It was a clear move toward monarchy, and in keeping with the shift, Napoleon's face began to appear on French coins.

Yet Napoleon continued to identify himself with the French Revolution, and the right continued to plot against him. In 1804, the British abetted the largest anti-Napoleonic conspiracy yet, which involved two prominent generals from the revolutionary era and a swashbuckling counterrevolutionary guerrilla leader from western France named Georges Cadoudal. They planned to capture or kill Napoleon and to have one of the generals take power in preparation for a return of the Bourbon dynasty. But Fouché's efficient counterintelligence service quickly uncovered the plot and arrested the principals. Cadoudal was executed; one of the generals died in prison—by strangling himself, so the guards claimed. Napoleon, determined to mete out another, exemplary punishment to the right, then authorized French troops to cross the border into German territory and seize a prince of the House of Bourbon, the Duke d'Enghien, who had opposed Napoleon without taking a direct part in the plot. After a quick court-martial, the duke was shot by a firing squad. Europeans who had barely noticed Napoleon's slaughter of thousands of Turkish soldiers in Jaffa could not contain their outrage over this judicial murder of a single Bourbon, and the action indeed hugely harmed Napoleon's reputation outside France. According to a quip attributed to several different high French officials, it was not just a crime but a blunder. Napoleon himself insisted, the day after the execution, "I am a statesman. I am the French Revolution and I will uphold it."

It is important to stress that while the regime created between 1799 and 1804 was authoritarian, illiberal, and undemocratic, it was not, despite the execution of d'Enghien, exceptionally arbitrary or bloodthirsty. Fouché's networks of spies and informers and his severe censorship system might seem to recall the worst dictatorships of the twentieth century. But unlike those regimes, Napoleon's France had no gulag and no concentration camps. Throughout Napoleon's fifteen years in power, there were few political executions, and the rate of political imprisonment remained tiny by modern standards. Napoleon in fact reversed some of the harsher measures taken by the Directory during the military crisis of 1798–99 and allowed émigrés who had fled France during the Revolution to return. Many of the leading French authors of the day—Benjamin Constant, Germaine de Staël, François-René de Chateaubriand—ferociously attacked Napoleon in print at one time or another without losing their lives or their liberty. Chateaubriand compared Napoleon to Nero, and while Napoleon threatened to kill him for the insult, the writer actually suffered nothing worse than banishment to his country estate. Even an act of high treason by Napoleon's most important minister, Talleyrand, resulted only in the man's dismissal and banishment (and a choice epithet—Napoleon called him "shit in a silk stocking"). Napoleon was no Stalin.

It was against this authoritarian but not murderous backdrop that Napoleon's collaborators set about erecting his new regime. Their goal, in keeping with his political vision, was to create a state that was in thrall to a single central power but oversaw society efficiently, fairly, and peacefully. It would respect the principle of equality before the law. But it would also promote social stability, by defending the rights of property-holders and of fathers and husbands.

Institutionally, the single most important innovation was the office of prefect. The French Revolution had replaced France's traditional provinces (Brittany, Normandy, Provence, etc.) with eighty-three smaller "departments," whose number later swelled with wartime annexations. Under Napoleon, each department acquired a single executive prefect, responsible for executing the laws, acting as the agent of the central government, and managing a small stable of subprefects. Though the departments retained their own elected bodies, the prefecture guaranteed that no intermediary bodies with real authority would come between individual citizens and the central state.

Napoleon and his collaborators also expanded the practice (which dated back to the Old Regime) of drawing virtually all top civil servants from a handful of elite "corps," whose members were recruited from equally elite "grandes écoles" ("great schools"), most notably the École Polytechnique. The system, in theory meritocratic and apolitical, in practice favored men from wealthy families and made it virtually impossible for others to work their way up to top positions. It therefore helped to solidify a new social elite of so-called notables, bound by family ties to the highest levels of state service. (These notables were themselves sometimes nicknamed the "masses of granite.") The system also tended to prize abstract intellectual skills above concrete experience. One of the most important corps staffed the new, unelected State Council, which advised the executive on legal matters and acted as an administrative court overseeing the government as a whole. The Council and the rest of the administrative system still exist today in much the same form. Most recent French presidents and prime ministers have belonged to elite corps in the civil service.

Underpinning the reform process was an initiative that would have worldwide influence: a new, streamlined law code. Old Regime France had been governed by a byzantine web of different and often conflicting codes, including hundreds of separate "customary" ones (supposedly derived from long-standing popular customs). The revolutionaries had tried to devise a new, simpler law code, without much success. But soon after taking power, Napoleon directed Cambacérès and the State Council to complete the task, and he chaired many of the discussions himself. The First Consul, well versed in geometry from his training in the artillery, dreamed, in his own words, of "reducing all of law to simple geometric demonstrations." In the event, he settled for an admirably clear, concise distillation of Roman law principles as they had developed in France. (The Romans envisioned law as "written reason," applied from above, rather than as the accumulated legal experience of a community.)

What became formally known after 1807 as the "Code Napoléon" was valid throughout the length and breadth of the country. It confirmed the French revolutionary principle of equality before the law—including the end of noble privilege—and the rights of all children to a share of an inheritance, an innovation that fundamentally changed patterns of French property-holding. It also placed strong guarantees on the rights of fathers and husbands, sharply cutting back on the right to divorce and on women's property rights in general. Among other things, the code stipulated that married women could not publish books or articles without their husband's permission—a provision not fully abolished until 1965(!). The Code also firmly defended property rights. The Code itself has been widely copied, including in many European countries and nearly all of Latin America.

Napoleon did keep in place the Revolution's direct taxes on income and wealth, but he also revived, under new names, some of the Old Regime's hated excise and sales taxes. The Consulate began an overhaul of French education and, in particular, created a new system of elite high schools (*lycées*), designed above all to prepare a small minority of mostly propertied men for careers in state service. Napoleon founded the Legion of Honor to recognize the citizenry's meritorious achievements.

There was one other, crucial measure taken in the name of stability. Since the Terror, and the attempts by men like Fouché to wipe out Christianity in France, the Catholic Church had remained in limbo in the country. The vast majority of the French remained Catholic in theory (Protestants and Jews represented well under 5 percent of the population), and many regions were strongly devout. On the other hand a large proportion of the social, political, and military elite, including Napoleon himself, were freethinking and anticlerical. Still, Napoleon realized that social peace required an accommodation with religion. Long negotiations with Pope Pius VII resulted in a formal "Concordat" with Rome, signed in 1801. It limited the size of the French clergy and bound its members tightly to the French state, which would henceforth pay their salaries. The "Organic Articles" strictly limited the pope's authority in France. The Concordat did not formally reestablish Catholicism as an official state church but did recognize it as "the religion of the great majority of the French people." The agreement also confirmed one of the Revolution's most important reforms. Starting in 1789, the government had expropriated the Catholic Church's vast landholdings in France and sold them off, in many cases to wealthy peasants. The guarantee of the purchasers' rights to this land, which the Napoleonic Code again reaffirmed, helped to solidify the peasantry's economic position for the next century and a half, while also turning it in a politically conservative direction.

There was still more: the Consulate also created France's first successful national bank and stabilized the currency. It did not fully embrace modern forms of state accounting, and down to 1814 Napoleon's regime remained reliant, like the Old Regime before it, on wealthy financiers who ran part of the French financial apparatus virtually as a private business. But after a decade of revolutionary upheavals a large measure of economic stability was nonetheless restored.

Overall, it is certainly possible to exaggerate the effectiveness of the Consulate's domestic reforms. However impressive, and apparently rational the structures, the façades concealed considerable jerry-rigging, revivals of corrupt Old Regime practices, and sheer bureaucratic waste. Soon after Napoleon's fall, an Interior Ministry official memorably complained: "Of 500 mayors to whom a prefect writes on any kind of measure at all, 200 execute it, 150 answer that they are executing it without actually doing so, and 150 do not respond at all." Napoleonic officials often proved less good at governing than at snooping, and at producing ever more complex forms of paperwork, many of which are still (alas) familiar to anyone who lives in France. Honoré de Balzac, wonderfully, called the regime "the nosiest, most meticulous, most scribbling, red-tape mongering, list-making, controlling, verifying, cautious, and finally just the most cleaning-lady of administrations—past, present or future."

Even so, and even with the authoritarian repression and rigged plebiscites, it is clear that the population generally supported both the reforms and Napoleon's rule in general—the propertied classes above all. The First Consul had brought order to the country, secured the civic equality promised by the Revolution, and obtained a victorious peace within expanded borders. If the price to be paid was submission to Tocqueville's "immense tutelary power," most of the French, for the moment, were willing to pay. Napoleon's prefect of the Department of the Lower Seine summed up the situation in 1802. The department, he wrote, has "has an excellent public spirit, because there reigns here a great political immobility and a great movement towards domestic concerns. When a people has made a wise and serious delegation of public powers, it has nothing better to do than to occupy itself with other matters."

Even as he proceeded with his internal reforms, Napoleon believed that in order to survive economically, France ultimately needed to rebuild its overseas colonial empire. With the last French forces in Egypt having surrendered in 1801, he instead turned his attention across the Atlantic and particularly toward the former jewel of the French empire, Saint-Domingue, which had previously produced 40 percent of Europe's sugar and half its coffee and accounted for a large share of French exports. Following the massive slave rebellion of 1791, bouts of civil war, and British and Spanish incursions, Saint-Domingue was in turmoil when Napoleon took power. The most powerful figure in the island, the charismatic black general Toussaint Louverture, acknowledged overall French authority but demanded considerable autonomy. In planning to reassert French authority in the region, Napoleon first engineered the return to France of the territorially massive but sparsely developed Louisiana Territory in North America, which had been ceded to Spain in 1763. Napoleon saw it principally as a supply depot for the more profitable Caribbean colony.

In 1801, Napoleon sent a military expedition commanded by his brother-in-law Victor-Emmanuel Leclerc to reassert direct French authority on Saint-Domingue itself, to reestablish slavery, and to crush Toussaint if he refused to accept a renewed colonial order. The expedition arrived at the end of 1801 and met with some initial successes. With the help of black allies, the French captured Toussaint and sent him back to France, where he died in captivity. But the war quickly turned into a struggle for independence. Leclerc vowed a campaign of extermination and committed large-scale atrocities, including the use of man-eating dogs to hunt down black victims. But an epidemic of yellow fever decimated the French troops and killed Leclerc himself. Finally, in 1803 the French withdrew from the island, allowing for the resistance forces to establish the independent black state of Haiti the following year. With Napoleon's plans for the region in ruins, he then, without much deliberation, sold the Louisiana Territory to the United States, allowing President Thomas Jefferson to double the size of the young American republic at a single stroke. The French overseas empire again found itself reduced to little more than a string of small islands, including the Caribbean sugar colonies of Martinique and Guadeloupe. There the French did indeed successfully reestablish slavery, which the French revolutionaries had formally abolished in 1794. It was one of Napoleon's greatest crimes and was not reversed until the coming of the Second Republic to France in 1848.

The failure of the colonial venture was a major humiliation for Napoleon. The French, however, gave it relatively little attention, because well before news of the final defeat reached Europe, the frail Peace of Amiens with Great Britain had broken down. After just a year without hostilities in Europe, France again found itself in a war that would soon pit it against a broad coalition of European states. Indeed, this new war would take place on a larger scale than ever before and would soon very much overshadow not just the Saint-Domingue expedition but the domestic achievements of the Consulate as well.

The resumption of hostilities had been overdetermined. For one thing, Napoleon himself clearly believed that his rule depended on continual military success. "A First Consul is not like kings…who see their states as an inheritance," he remarked in May 1803. "He needs brilliant deeds, and therefore war." His European victories since taking power, and his domestic successes, had done nothing to diminish a self-confidence that had long ago passed the boundaries of hubris. The domestic successes encouraged Napoleon as well, because they allowed him to mobilize France's massive resources for war more efficiently than ever before in the country's history. But France's adversaries bore their own share of the blame. Most European monarchs still regarded the French Republic as, at bottom, an illegitimate regime. They also saw France's expansion as upsetting the balance of power that had prevailed before the French Revolution, and they yearned for an opportunity to reverse it. The British press denounced Napoleon at every turn, and it was the British government that formally violated the terms of the peace by refusing to evacuate the island of Malta.

Adding to these factors, the cascade of territorial and political changes over the preceding decade, which dwarfed anything seen in the previous century, provided countless potential flashpoints. For instance, because France had annexed so much German territory, Napoleon now saw it as having vital strategic interests throughout the fragmented German federation known as the Holy Roman Empire. In 1803, he helped bring about a large-scale reorganization of German territory that abolished many of that empire's tiny statelets. He also annexed additional territories in Italy. His consolidation of states in both Germany and Italy would outlast his rule and help to pave the way for the eventual national unifications of both countries in the later nineteenth century. But what for him seemed a simple consolidation of France's position on the map struck his adversaries as pure aggression. Disputes multiplied, with the British objecting to the presence of French troops in the Netherlands and then holding onto Malta. Napoleon himself, having little understanding of the operations of a free press, castigated the British government for not censoring the British newspapers' vicious attacks on him.

The British finally declared war in the spring of 1803. They seized French ships in British ports; in response, Napoleon took the even more radical step of arresting several thousand Britons who had taken advantage of the Peace of Amiens to reacquaint themselves with France (and its luxury goods). He also completed a reorganization of the French land armies into a massive force christened the Grande Armée, composed of a flexible series of distinct corps, each made up of twenty to thirty thousand men—a system that has formed the basis for the organization of the most important modern military forces. The army was staffed mostly by long-serving veterans, trained in the revolutionary style for massive attacks in column, supported by swarms of skirmishers. This system made for a hugely effective force, and Napoleon deployed it in a series of camps near the town of Boulogne on the coast of the English Channel, preparing for an invasion of England. He ordered the construction of some twenty-five hundred gunboats, barges, and landing crafts.

It was in this context of renewed war that Napoleon took a step that ended the Consulate and forever changed his relationship to his country, to Europe, and to his image in history. He literally put a crown on his head. The constitution of 1802 had already made him a monarch of sorts, giving him office for life, with the right to choose his own successor. Yet just a year later, a government pamphlet was insisting that "to better save the fatherland, Bonaparte must agree to become king of the Revolution." In early 1804, speaker after speaker arose in the tame Tribunate to demand that he become not a king—a title far too redolent of the Old Regime—but an emperor. "What other glory does not eclipse and efface itself before that of the incomparable Hero who has conquered them all...and created another universe for us?" Yet another constitution, Napoleon's third, was duly submitted to a rigged plebiscite and overwhelmingly approved.

This move to monarchy grew, in one sense, directly out of Napoleon's immense self-regard and social conservatism. But that was not the whole story. It is worth remembering that even more than a decade after the French Revolution, Europe remained dominated by conservative monarchies whose leaders saw the specter of Robespierre behind every symbol of the French Republic. To have them treat him as an honorable equal, Napoleon genuinely believed that he had to become a monarch himself. And the transformation of Consul Bonaparte into Emperor Napoleon I did not mark a complete break with the Revolution, even if the new constitution failed to acknowledge the key revolutionary principle of popular sovereignty. Napoleon did not take the title "Emperor of France," implying in some way that he owned the country, but rather "Emperor of the French." The official act creating the empire stated, a little confusingly, that "the government of the Republic is entrusted to an emperor." The Napoleonic Code and the principle of civic equality remained in place. Napoleon clearly wished to present himself as a man of the center, reconciling the Old Regime and the Revolution in his own person.

Symbolism, however, is a powerful thing. On December 2, 1804, a sumptuous coronation ceremony took place in Notre Dame Cathedral, which the Revolution, just eleven years before, had stripped of its gold and turned into a "Temple of Reason." Pope Pius VII himself took part, so as to highlight the comparison Napoleon wanted to draw between himself and another emperor of the West: Charlemagne (crowned by a pope a thousand years before). Napoleon dressed in a magnificent heavy ermine-lined robe of crimson velvet, decorated with a symbol taken from the tombs of France's ancient Merovingian dynasty: golden bees. He held a scepter used by medieval kings and took a newly forged crown from the pope's hands and placed it on his own head. Josephine—the new empress—wore a robe similar to her husband's, and the entire Bonaparte clan now assumed the position of a royal family. The painter David, who had previously rendered French revolutionaries as the successors to the heroes of the Roman Republic and the murdered radical demagogue Jean-Paul Marat as a Christ-like martyr, recorded the event in one of his most lavish tableaux. His student Jean-Auguste-Dominique Ingres painted the new emperor in his coronation robes as an eerie medieval icon, flat, pale and expressionless. A critic claimed Ingres was trying "to push back art four centuries."

A new monarchy required a new nobility, and within a few years Napoleon would start to lavish titles on his followers and amalgamate them with the nobility of the Old Regime (to whom he showed increasing favor). Napoleon's own family members received noble and princely titles, while his close aide Berthier became Prince of Neuchâtel. Fouché, the former atheist revolutionary, was transformed into the Duke of Otranto. Talleyrand, the Old Regime noble turned revolutionary, emerged as Prince of Benevento. The new nobility did not enjoy the legal privileges of the old one (including exemptions from many forms of taxation). Yet its creation, following on the coronation ceremony, sent a powerful signal that in the French Empire, all people were not, in fact, truly equal.

The transformation of the French Republic into an empire also sent another signal. The Revolution had marked, in important

6. Napoleon used the arts to help legitimate his new imperial title. This stern and deliberately anachronistic portrait of him in his coronation robes by Jean-Auguste-Dominique Ingres emphasized the resemblance to medieval rulers.

ways, the birth of French nationalism (indeed, of modern nationalism full stop). Whereas the monarchs of the Old Regime had tolerated a great diversity of customs, laws, and even languages among their subjects, the revolutionaries believed that democracy could only function in a cohesive, uniform nation-state. Among other things, they devised ambitious plans to teach standard French to the millions of French citizens who spoke Breton, German, Basque, or one of many Romance dialects as their maternal language. But the expanded borders of 1804 contained millions more people who had not considered themselves French before the Revolution and mostly did not speak French at all. Would Napoleon now continue the revolutionary project, and attempt to incorporate these people as well into a cohesive French nation-state? The creation of an "empire" suggested an alternate path: a multinational federation of sorts, with an official language (French) and uniform laws (the Code Napoléon) but otherwise tolerant of cultural diversity. An "empire" was also infinitely expandable in ways a nation-state was not, signaling that Napoleon's ambitions as a conqueror had, with the resumption of war, increased by yet another degree of magnitude. As he would later confide to Benjamin Constant, "I wanted to rule the world—who wouldn't have, in my place?"

Even amid the glitter of the coronation ceremony, one glimpse of the older, less pompous Napoleon could still be found. As he stood in his heavy robes, under the great vaulted ceiling of Notre Dame, scepter in hand, he turned to his brother Joseph, now dressed as a prince, and whispered, grinning: "If Papa could see us now." But in coming years, this older Napoleon would be seen less and less.

Chapter 4
The emperor, 1804–1812

Perhaps because Napoleon mythologized himself so insistently, it is easy to imagine him as a series of figures from Greek mythology. For the early Napoleon there is Hercules, accomplishing apparently impossible feats and sweeping out the Augean stables of French government with his consul's broom. For the late Napoleon, one thinks of Prometheus: the titan chained to his South Atlantic rock, pecked at by English vultures. And for the emperor in his heyday, the figure that comes irresistibly to mind is Icarus, soaring higher, higher, and higher still, until suddenly his wings fall apart and he plummets from the sky. Except that in Napoleon's case it is not the heat of the sun that prompts his fall but the howling chill of the Russian winter.

But such images are deceptive, and none more so than the last. One can certainly write Napoleon's career between 1804 and 1812 as a series of battles won (Austerlitz, Jena, Friedland, Borodino) or enemy capitals triumphantly entered (Vienna, Berlin, Madrid, Moscow). One can also write it by tracing the expanding borders of the First Empire on the map. By 1812 they extended across northern Germany to the borders of Denmark, down the Italian peninsula to Rome, and across the Pyrenees to Barcelona. The rest of Italy and Spain were satellite states, along with Poland's "Duchy of Warsaw," and the "Confederation of the Rhine" in Germany.

A shrunken Prussia and Austria had become subservient allies. By these standards, the period looked like one of steady ascent.

Napoleon certainly relished his victories and his conquests, which only confirmed his belief in his unique, transcendent destiny. But in truth, as the years passed after 1804, on almost every level he controlled events less and less. The new political and military forces unleashed by the French Revolution, which had made possible his astonishing conquests and reforms, did not allow him to consolidate and preserve them. Instead, a different geopolitical dynamic took shape. On the level of grand strategy, Napoleon felt increasingly forced into incessant war and annexation, above all because of his inability to overcome his greatest and most supremely frustrating enemy, Great Britain. On the battlefield the contending armies grew exponentially, becoming far more difficult to manage—and more and more of the battles themselves were either lost or barely won, and at a frightful cost. And the conquered territories refused to stay conquered, with insurgents dragging the French into a series of painful and draining guerrilla wars. In retrospect, the bloated boundaries of the empire in 1812 look less like the markers of a new Roman Empire than the skin of a bubble about to burst. This trajectory was not immediately apparent when Napoleon crowned himself emperor. Indeed, the next two years saw him win some of his greatest triumphs. But they also saw two key setbacks that over time would tell more and more heavily against him.

These setbacks both involved naval power, and the fatal disadvantages France had at sea in comparison with Great Britain. Napoleon could build ships, and put men in sailors' uniforms, but developing a powerful navy required another ingredient—expertise—and here France fell terribly short. Even the lowest ranking sailor in the age of sail required far more skill and experience than an ordinary land soldier in order to serve effectively. Officers required years of specialized training in order to navigate and maneuver ships moved by dozens of different sails and armed with scores of cannon. British naval officers generally started when still young boys. Throughout the "long eighteenth century" (1688–1815), the British navy needed forcibly to "impress," or forcibly conscript, nearly half its sailors—but it could do so very largely from its own merchant marine and thereby at least acquired experienced seamen. France, with a far less developed maritime tradition, simply could not match the British in this crucial arena. In some Napoleonic naval battles, fully half the French sailors had never been to sea before. France also suffered from severe shortages of naval stores.

The deficit first made itself felt in Napoleon's aborted attempt to invade England. The army assembled on the Channel coast in 1803-4 was perhaps the most impressive yet seen in Europe.

7. Europe in 1812.

Eventually numbering more than two hundred thousand men, it was seasoned, highly trained, well-motivated, and well-equipped. Its objective—England—lay barely thirty miles away. The English Channel, Napoleon claimed, was "a mere ditch, to be crossed the moment anyone has the courage to try." Yet for all his bravado, the ditch might as well have been the Pacific, because despite constructing an invasion flotilla of some twenty-five hundred barges and small craft, Napoleon had no way to get his men safely across. The largest part of the French navy itself was bottled up in the Mediterranean, and without its covering presence the British would have quickly reduced the flotilla to flotsam. In 1805, French admiral Villeneuve finally managed to bring his fleet out into the Atlantic but quickly retreated to Cádiz, on the Atlantic coast of France's ally Spain. Meanwhile, Russia and Austria were joining the new anti-French coalition (referred to as the "Third Coalition"). To meet this new threat, Napoleon withdrew his army from around Boulogne and marched toward Germany. The chance to defeat England decisively had, for the moment, been lost.

Then, in October, France's naval fate was sealed by the second setback. On Napoleon's insistence, Villeneuve took the French and Spanish fleets out to sea. On October 21 they confronted Admiral Nelson and the British Royal Navy off Spain's Cape Trafalgar. Villeneuve had a quarter more ships than the British, but British naval expertise counted more heavily. While Villeneuve used the classic technique of assembling his ships in one long easily controlled line, Nelson organized his into two great flexible and maneuverable columns—a feat requiring all the naval expertise he and his men could muster—and sailed directly into the Franco-Spanish line, breaking it. Nelson himself was killed in the battle, but Villeneuve lost more than half his ships and thousands of sailors. From then on, Napoleon could never again hope to challenge British control of the high seas.

Even so, for several years, the twin disappointments did not seem to affect Napoleon's "destiny." In this classic confrontation of "whale" and "elephant" between Britain and France, the elephant might have no chance of ruling the waves but could stomp the land to its heart's content. And in 1805–6, Napoleon's forces stomped the continent of Europe more decisively than any army had done since the days of Julius Caesar.

On August 23, 1805, the emperor began moving his massive Grande Armée away from the English Channel and toward central Europe. Some days, despite carrying packs weighing as much as eighty pounds, the soldiers marched thirty-five miles. At the end of September they crossed the Rhine and in mid-October, after a series of brilliant maneuvers, surrounded the main Austrian army in the southern German city of Ulm. Austria's General Mack could not break out and, after three days of relentless French fire, surrendered the city. Nearly half the Austrians became casualties or prisoners, leaving the French free to follow the Danube River downstream for nearly 450 miles with little serious opposition. On November 13, the Grande Armée entered Vienna, the Austrian capital.

The campaign was not over, however. The remaining Austrian forces, accompanied by their emperor, met up with a larger Russian army to the north of the capital in what is now the Czech Republic. In the Russian camp was none other than Tsar Alexander I, the ambitious twenty-eight year-old grandson of Catherine the Great. On December 2, exactly a year after his coronation, Napoleon confronted the allied force near the Czech village of Austerlitz. On both sides, leading generals urged caution, but Napoleon and Alexander both insisted on fighting, and it was here that Napoleon won perhaps his most brilliant victory. After surveying the field the day before, he deliberately weakened his right flank in the hope of drawing a massive attack by the allies that would leave their center vulnerable. In the evening, in a jovial mood, he dined on his preferred field dish of potatoes and onions (*not* chicken Marengo!) and reminisced with his subordinates about Egypt. The next morning the allies obligingly took his bait, pressing forward hard against his right. In midmorning he ordered a crucial counterattack by Marshal Soult's divisions, up onto the strategic Pratzen Heights, and gave the men a triple ration of liquor to encourage their boldness. Hidden by fog, they charged up the slope, and then, in one of the grand moments of the Napoleonic legend, just as they reached the crucial position, the mist dispersed, and the "sun of Austerlitz" revealed them to the stunned Russians.

By the end of the day, the French had completed a ruthless destruction of the enemy forces. As Russian troops retreated across frozen lakes, the ice cracked, possibly as a result of deliberate French cannon fire. "We saw thousands of Russians, along with their many horses, cannons and wagons, slowly sink into the abyss," a French general later claimed. More than 130 captured Russian cannon were melted down and cast into a giant victory column that still stands today in the Place Vendôme in Paris (although the Commune of 1871 briefly tore it down).

The decisive defeat at Austerlitz left Austria vulnerable and with no choice but to seek peace yet again. (Russia, despite the smashing of its army, held out until 1807.) The resulting Treaty of Pressburg brought yet more major changes to European politics and borders. Napoleon had already transformed France's satellite republic in northern Italy into the "Kingdom of Italy," with himself wearing the Iron Crown supposedly used by Charlemagne and Josephine's son Eugène de Beauharnais as his viceroy. Now this kingdom annexed the former lands of the Republic of Venice. Napoleon also forced Austria's emperor, Francis, to renounce the crown of the Holy Roman Empire and to dissolve that creaky but still-significant union, which descended from Charlemagne's empire and claimed the succession of the Roman Caesars. In its place Napoleon oversaw the reorganization of many German states into the new subservient Confederation of the Rhine. And after decisively defeating yet another coalition member, the southern Italian Kingdom of Naples, in early 1806, he threw the

Bourbon dynasty off its throne and put in their place his older brother Joseph. Now the Bonaparte family directly ruled most of Italy and directly or indirectly controlled most of Germany as well.

This new wave of French expansion meant that Napoleon's vision of authoritarian and egalitarian government was spreading outward from France to transform public life across much of the continent. Not only the areas annexed directly to France but also those under strong French influence would, for the most part, see the introduction of the Napoleonic Code, and France's principles of civic equality, before the decade was out. Discriminatory laws that had closed most professions to Jews, and even limited their residence to enclosed ghettoes, were repealed. The power of established Christian churches was reduced and some church lands were confiscated. The government heavily promoted the French language. In fact, after 1805 Napoleon came to believe that he could make all of Europe into a Consular France writ large, with the sort of unity unseen since the days of Rome. Fouché in his memoirs remembered the emperor saying: "We need a European law code, a European supreme court, a single currency, the same weights and measures, the same laws; I must make all the peoples of Europe into a single people, and Paris, the capital of the world." It was a stunning ambition, and, to his credit, in the process Napoleon was ready to give full equal rights in his empire to those non-French Europeans willing to accept the terms of his new order. During the decade of his imperial rule the numbers of imperial officials born outside France grew steadily.

Yet the process did not go anywhere nearly as smoothly as Napoleon wished, especially in rural areas. "The absence of almost all civilization... indicates the savage morality of this country," one administrator would write at the height of the empire, not from a distant colony but from the mountains of central Italy, within easy reach of Rome. In many cases, the administrators ended up applying French norms by force, using soldiers and paramilitary forces. Especially in the Catholic lands of southern Europe, the peasantry saw the French not as emancipatory agents of "civilization" but as brutal colonizers.

Meanwhile, Napoleon's gift of a throne to his older brother did not exactly send an encouraging message about the spread of revolutionary values. "Well, Prince," runs the first line of Tolstoy's *War and Peace*, which begins in 1805, "so Genoa and Lucca are now just family estates of the Buonapartes." Soon, many observers felt that all of Europe was coming to fit precisely this description. Napoleon would make one younger brother (Jerome) king of Westphalia in Germany, and another (Louis) king of Holland. After first sending Joseph to Naples, he transferred him two years later to Spain, handing Naples on to brother-in-law Joachim Murat. Sister Elisa became the reigning grand duchess of Parma, in Italy. In the clan, only the impetuous third son, Lucien, to whom Napoleon owed the most (he had, after all, saved the day and possibly even Napoleon's life during the coup of the Eighteenth Brumaire), remained a revolutionary at heart and spurned imperial honors.

Imperial expansion, meanwhile, soon began to produce the sorts of conflict that threatened to undermine the entire Napoleonic enterprise. Napoleon himself was not blind to the problem. Soon after dispatching Joseph to Naples, he wrote to the new king: "Include in your calculations the fact that within a fortnight, more or less, you will have an insurrection. It is an event that constantly occurs in occupied countries." But Napoleon probably had in mind nothing more than the sort of disorganized protests he had so ruthlessly squelched in northern Italy ten years earlier. What happened in Naples proved much more difficult to contain. A network of guerrilla fighters still survived from the kingdom's earlier brush with French invaders in the late 1790s. The British navy, from a base in Sicily, supplied the insurgents from the sea, and throughout 1806 a series of French generals desperately tried to extinguish one rebel brushfire after another in difficult, mountainous terrain. Their opponents were not exactly nationalist freedom-fighters. Going by nicknames such as "the Executioner," "the Bizarre," and "Brother Devil," they extorted arms, money, property, and even women from the local population and tortured and killed many of their prisoners, often in exceptionally gruesome ways. Their own ally, British general John Moore, called them "mafia…a lawless banditti, enemies to all governments whatever… fit to plunder and murder, but much too dastardly to face an enemy." To suppress them the French resorted to atrocities of their own. In August 1806, Marshal André Masséna ordered the sacking of the Calabrian town of Lauria, where at least 734 men, women, and children were killed, mostly in cold blood. Along the road south from the town, the French displayed the heads of 184 insurgents in iron cages. Slowly, these methods, and the increasing use of local auxiliaries, did restore order. In November, after long and dramatic chases through the Appenine Mountains, the forces of Major Joseph-Léopold Hugo (father of Victor) captured and executed the most successful of the guerrilla leaders. But small-scale rebellions continued to flare up, and the conflict dragged on in one form or another for four more years.

Yet even as the French struggled to absorb their Italian conquests, Napoleon's ambitions in Germany helped trigger yet another bout of major warfare in central Europe. The Kingdom of Prussia had not fought France since 1795. But in the summer of 1806, concerned about the extension of French influence in Germany, King Friedrich Wilhelm III formed an alliance with the tsar, who was still at war with Napoleon and still smarting from his humiliation at Austerlitz. For Prussia in particular, this "Fourth Coalition" (including Britain as well) was a grievous mistake, which would soon lead to yet another devastating French victory. Yet the new war gave further evidence of how, even as Napoleon seemed to achieve his greatest military successes, he was finding it more difficult to control events.

On receiving Prussia's ultimatum to withdraw beyond the Rhine, Napoleon led a force of 180,000 men into Germany, and on

October 14, 1806, it confronted the Prussian army in two simultaneous battles at Jena and Auerstadt. The Prussian army had a fearsome reputation, dating back to the days of Frederick the Great in the eighteenth century, but in truth its leaders were old and ponderous, their tactics old-fashioned, and their ordinary soldiers—for the most part conscripts, mercenaries, and former prisoners of war—poorly motivated. Despite some errors on Napoleon's part, the mobile, flexible French force won both battles decisively. And, even more ruthlessly than after his past victories, he set about utterly destroying the army he had just defeated. Not only did he take every major Prussian fortress; of the 171,000 soldiers sent into action against him his armies killed, wounded, or took prisoner all but six thousand. In early November, he marched in triumph into Berlin. In nearby Potsdam, he stopped to see the tomb of Frederick the Great and stood at the entrance, silent and brooding, for ten minutes, before making off with the king's sword and decorations. The philosopher Georg Wilhelm Friedrich Hegel, who later claimed to have seen Napoleon ride beneath his window in Jena, was moved to write of the events as nothing less than a turning point in the history of humanity: "The connecting bonds of the world are dissolved and have collapsed like images in a dream." He called Napoleon "the world-soul... who, sitting here astride a horse, reaches out across the world and dominates it."

Indeed, in the middle years of the decade, praise for Napoleon's apparently superhuman genius flowed in a torrent, from some of the greatest minds in Europe. The German writer Johann Wolfgang von Goethe had an interview with the emperor in 1808, and it convinced him of Napoleon's "state of continued illumination... indeed we see at his side divine protection and a constant fortune." The future social theorist Henri de Saint-Simon insisted that a monument to Napoleon would have to recognize him not simply as the equal of Alexander, Caesar, and Charlemagne but also of Plato, Aristotle and Descartes. The future poet Lord Byron kept a bust of Napoleon in his room at Harrow.

Beethoven planned to dedicate his Third Symphony to Napoleon, although he changed his mind after the proclamation of the empire. Napoleon himself was all too happy to believe this slathering of praise.

And yet, even after smashing Prussia, a definitive triumph remained frustratingly distant. Even after the fall of Berlin, the Russians, along with a few surviving Prussian units, refused to yield. Napoleon pursued them eastward, in the depths of winter, into East Prussia (now part of Russia), to the town of Eylau. There in February 1807 he fought one of his most horrific battles, at fifteen degrees below zero. Over two days the armies battered each other, and while Napoleon was left in possession of the field, he gained little but heaps of frozen, mutilated corpses. "What a massacre, and without a result," moaned one of his greatest marshals, Michel Ney. By this point in his career Napoleon, always the deft propagandist, had turned his bombastic but thrilling military dispatches into something of an art form, always boasting of the élan with which the French had overcome their enemies. But after Eylau the suddenly sober dispatch called the battle a "horror." Antoine-Jean Gros, who had previously painted Napoleon as the dashing hero of Arcola, produced a frightening tableau of Eylau that placed the gray-faced emperor on horseback, the town burning behind him, and grotesque cadavers in the foreground. Though Eylau was not a defeat, it was the largest battle yet that had not gone Napoleon's way.

A few months later, Napoleon did manage to crush the Russians at the Battle of Friedland, and he followed it up with a triumphant meeting with Tsar Alexander on a gaudily decorated raft in the middle of the Niemen River, on the Russian border, near the town of Tilsit. Napoleon was magnanimous to the tsar, calling him a brother and urging him to sign a treaty of alliance. He was far harsher to the Prussian king, whom he left waiting on the shore, in another deliberate act of humiliation. He stripped Prussia of fully half its territory and subjects and reduced its army to a token force. Coming on top of the military defeat, the treaty lit a fire of Prussian resentment against France that would smolder long after the end of the Napoleonic wars.

It would seem that Napoleon's star had risen even higher. Yet his most powerful enemy remained a stubbornly potent threat. True, with its coalition members all defeated, Great Britain in some ways felt harder pressed than ever. The Romantic poet William Wordsworth wrote anxiously in late 1806: "We are left, or shall be left, alone; / The last that dare to struggle with the Foe." But in truth, the Royal Navy not only kept the British secure in their islands but posed a continuing and deadly economic threat to Napoleon by cutting France and its allies off from the networks of global trade that for more than half a century had served as key motors of European economic growth. If the "elephant" could not break the maritime stranglehold of the "whale," eventually it would suffocate, and Napoleon knew this.

Yet he had few good options for countering the threat. After Trafalgar, he had no hope of beating the British navy at sea, and the likelihood of a new peace agreement was small as well. The British government, supported by most (although not all) of the British public, saw Napoleon as an insatiable, tyrannical conqueror—the "Corsican Ogre," to use the favorite sobriquet of the British press—and insisted that the war continue. Napoleon himself, therefore, believed he had little choice other than to try and turn the economic weapon back against Britain. For while the British wanted to blockade France, Britain itself was economically dependent on European markets, in which to sell manufactured goods as well as products brought from around the world on British ships. If the British could no longer trade in Europe, they might be forced to come to terms; so in November 1806 Napoleon issued a decree from Berlin closing French and allied ports to British goods. The British responded with so-called Orders in Council that not only reinforced the blockade of France but sharply restricted neutral shipping. Napoleon then retaliated with an even more ambitious decree issued in Milan that proclaimed the British isles themselves "in a state of blockade" and banned any trade at all between them and Europe. What became known as Napoleon's "Continental System" aimed at nothing less than Britain's economic overthrow.

Yet Europe has tens of thousands of miles of coastline and scores of major ports. Keeping British ships, and neutral ships trading with Britain, away from this vast expanse was a Sisyphean task. Napoleon could only hope to accomplish it by controlling every coastline state as closely as possible, and this objective in turn pushed him inexorably toward further expansion. In theory, this expansion might bring him closer to his ideal of European unification, but it did so on a hopelessly accelerated timetable as the empire's growth far outpaced its capacity to extend its administration, integrate new territories, and absorb new subjects. Impressive as it was from the outside, the empire was increasingly coming to resemble a skyscraper built in haste, without a proper foundation. And it did not help that Napoleon, after his victories of 1805–6, felt himself virtually invincible. Talleyrand, the only figure capable of perhaps steering the belligerent parties toward peace and restraining the emperor, resigned as foreign minister in 1807. He was later banished for conspiring with France's enemies in the hope of forcing Napoleon to make peace. (As Talleyrand's biographer Duff Cooper remarked, "this was treachery, but it was treachery upon a magnificent scale.")

The dangers of the strategy Napoleon chose made themselves felt almost immediately. The Kingdom of Portugal was one of Britain's most important allies and trading partners. In July 1807, even as he was meeting triumphantly with the tsar at Tilsit, Napoleon ordered the Portuguese to close their ports to British shipping; predictably, they refused. Napoleon therefore made plans for an invasion and for the eventual partition of Portugal into smaller states. In the second half of 1807, a twenty-eight-thousand-man French army under General Jean-Andoche Junot overcame weak

Portuguese resistance and occupied Lisbon, the capital, forcing the ruling family to flee to their colony of Brazil.

But keeping Portugal under control required the cooperation of the large country lying between it and France, namely Spain. In theory, Spain had been France's ally since 1796, but it was anything but a reliable one. Its king was the ineffective, mentally unstable Carlos IV, who had for many years effectively surrendered power to his ambitious and conniving favorite Manuel Godoy, who was also the lover of Queen Maria Luisa. Godoy had briefly conspired with Prussia until Napoleon's capture of Berlin sent him scurrying back to his French patron. And to make matters worse, Carlos's vain, twenty-three-year-old son and heir, Fernando, had conspired against both Godoy and the king, leading to his arrest in October 1807. Unsurprisingly, Napoleon had no confidence whatsoever in the Spanish government, and he finally decided to replace Spain's Bourbons with a Bonaparte.

The scenario played itself out in early 1808. Throughout the winter, Napoleon reinforced his army in Spain. On March 17, large-scale riots in favor of Prince Fernando took place at the royal residence of Aranjuez, forcing Godoy's resignation and the king's abdication. Soon afterward, Napoleon's brother-in-law Joachim Murat led a French army into Madrid, while across the country French troops took over Spanish fortresses. Napoleon summoned both Fernando and Carlos across the border to the southwestern France, and in a remarkable scene, bullied them both into abdicating in favor of his brother Joseph. Napoleon displayed nothing but contempt for the Spanish royals, writing of Fernando's "stupidity" and boasting to a Spanish counselor that "nations with a lot of friars are easy to subjugate—I've had experience with them." The French wrote a new, moderate constitution for Spain, and Joseph prepared to trade his throne in Naples for the more prestigious one in Madrid, with Murat replacing him in what was becoming a game of musical thrones.

In theory, Napoleon had now expanded his empire to include not just Iberia but also Spain and Portugal's vast overseas empires, which covered nearly all of Latin America and substantial colonies in Africa and Asia as well.

Reality, however, again proved frustrating—desperately so. The British navy kept the Iberian empires out of French hands. (Cut off from the metropole, they would begin to move toward independence.) More important, the attempt to place a Bonaparte on the Spanish throne triggered not just insurrections but a massive rebellion. In Madrid itself, Murat's men fought bloody street battles in the first days of May, and massacred hundreds of prisoners before restoring order. (The painter Francisco Goya immortalized the scenes in his brilliant works *Dos de Mayo* and *Tres de Mayo*.) Barcelona, Saragossa, Oviedo, Seville, and Valencia

8. To commemorate the successful Spanish resistance against Napoleon, the Spanish painter Francisco de Goya produced this phantasmagorical account of French troops executing Spanish patriots in Madrid in May 1808.

quickly joined in the rebellion, along with many smaller Spanish towns. On July 19 the regular Spanish army humiliated the French at the Battle of Baylen; soon afterward a British expeditionary force landed in Portugal, and helped recapture Lisbon from General Junot. These setbacks obliged Napoleon himself to come to Spain, at the head of an invading army. He won quick victories, secured Joseph's place on the throne, and imposed a new constitution on the country that made far fewer concessions to Spanish tradition and the Catholic Church.

Napoleon had spoken, in November 1806, of his enemies forcing him "to return, after so many years of civilization, to the principles that characterized the barbarism of the earliest ages of nations." He meant the weapons of economic strangulation deployed by the British. But in Spain his words took on new and sinister meaning as the war quickly descended into a level of brutality and horror that Europe had not seen since the Thirty Years War of the seventeenth century. In Saragossa, in central Spain, over the course of two sieges in 1808–9 the French army reduced much of the city to rubble with tens of thousands of explosive shells. The Spanish defenders refused to surrender, using "Guerra y cuchillo" (War to the knife) as their slogan. In the end the French had to take the city virtually house by house, through a maze of rubble. Witnesses spoke of streets strewn with corpses and corpses blasted out of their tombs in churches by the shelling. A typhus epidemic added to the horror, and by the time Saragossa finally surrendered in February 1809, at least fifty thousand Spaniards had died there.

The French could eventually capture most Spanish cities and towns, but the countryside was far more difficult to subdue. As in the Kingdom of Naples, guerrilla bands took shape—in fact, the modern word "guerrilla," Spanish for "little war," dates from precisely these events. As in Naples, the guerrilla leaders were part soldier, part bandit chieftain, and they took colorful nicknames: "The Potter," "The Grandfather," even "The Stick-in-the-Mud."

Drawing support partly from units of the Spanish regular army and partly from the peasantry, their mobile bands of horsemen specialized in hit-and-run attacks on French detachments on the move, and on isolated units. On November 20, 1807, for instance, 80 of the 719 French soldiers crossing the Sierra de Gata simply vanished. The most successful bands eventually numbered in the thousands and pinned down much larger numbers of the French. The French military governor of Navarre described the situation all too accurately when he lamented in a letter in 1810: "Unfortunately, in this region as in many others of Spain, our influence extends only as far as the range of our cannon.... The Spanish say quite rightly that our troops are plowing furrows in the water." Atrocities multiplied on both sides, with a "Spanish Catechism" of 1808 instructing the faithful that killing a Frenchman was no more a sin than killing a wild animal. A year later, a "junta" claiming loyalty to the imprisoned king Fernando called on every Spaniard to assault the enemy by any possible means. Napoleon, meanwhile, instructed his forces to take hostages and to execute four of the enemy for each of their own men killed. The guerrilla leader Espoz y Mina quickly announced he would employ the same calculus. A French officer later remembered that if he had carried out official decrees to the letter, "we would have had to put almost the entire population of the country to death."

Making matters even worse for Napoleon were the British. An expeditionary force based in Portugal and commanded by Sir Arthur Wellesley resisted successive attempts to retake Lisbon and conducted its own incursions into Spain, helping the guerrillas and the remnants of the Spanish royal army. Wellesley, a cautious but brilliant soldier, won a series of decisive victories over several of Napoleon's marshals, gaining him the title Lord Wellington. All in all, the war that became known as Napoleon's "Spanish ulcer" pinned down over three hundred thousand French soldiers between 1808 and 1812. The total number of French casualties probably exceeded 150,000.

Beyond bleeding the French of men and materiel, the Spanish conflict also encouraged Napoleon's enemies elsewhere. In the mountainous Austrian region of the Tyrol in 1809, a similarly vicious if smaller-scale insurrection broke out against France's ally Bavaria, ultimately forcing Napoleon to send in his own army. And the same year, the Austrian Empire took advantage of the Spanish chaos by declaring war on France yet again and forming the so-called Fifth Coalition. Napoleon hoped to crush the Austrians easily yet again, but the Battle of Aspern-Essling, in May, was an indecisive slaughterhouse reminiscent of Eylau. It took an intense and difficult campaign before he finally overcame the Austrians at Wagram in July.

Wagram was a decisive victory, but it illustrated yet another challenge facing Napoleon: the exponential expansion of battles in what was fast becoming an age of total war. Just sixty thousand soldiers had taken part in the Battle of Marengo, in 1800. At Austerlitz, in 1805, the number had swollen to 165,000. Wagram involved three hundred thousand, of whom eighty thousand were killed or wounded. Battles of this scope extended over far larger battlefields, making it far harder to bring dispersed units together for the decisive hammer blow, and far more difficult to wipe out a fleeing enemy. Not to mention the fact that Napoleon, now forty years old, was growing slower. The once nervously thin revolutionary was getting stout, and he suffered from increasingly severe urinary infections and a possible pituitary disorder, as well as what may have been mild epileptic fits. (Few people reached their forties in the early nineteenth century without accumulating a colorful collection of chronic ailments and parasites.) In 1805 he had confided to his valet: "One has only a certain time for war. I will be good for six years more; after that even I must cry halt."

The Fifth Coalition, beyond highlighting the empire's vulnerabilities, also brought a major change in Napoleon's personal life. After well over a decade of marriage, his feelings toward Josephine had grown both more complex and cooler.

The passion visible in his letters of the 1790s had melted into simple fondness. He had taken a series of mistresses, including a beautiful Polish noblewoman named Maria Walewska. Just as important, by 1809 Josephine was forty-six years old and no longer capable of bearing children. The creation of the empire had posed the inevitable problem of the succession, and while Napoleon had had formally adopted Josephine's son Eugène Beauharnais, he wanted a son of his own to succeed him. He initially hoped to marry a princess of the Russian royal family, but the tsar rebuffed him, and after the defeat of the Fifth Coalition, Napoleon instead negotiated an Austrian Habsburg bride as part of the peace settlement. The marriage to Josephine was duly dissolved, and in early 1810 Napoleon took as his new empress the plump, nineteen-year-old daughter of Emperor Francis of Austria. A year later she gave birth to the much desired heir, christened Napoleon after his father.

Napoleon might insist that he had married Maria Ludovica Leopoldina Franziska Therese Josepha Lucia von Habsburg-Lothringen to ensure the survival of his reforms. He could hardly deny, though, that she was the daughter of Europe's most conservative Catholic dynasty, or the grandniece of France's last queen, the infamous Marie Antoinette. Indeed, the marriage symbolized how Napoleon's regime, under the pressures of war and his own desire to pose as the first among imperial equals, was moving steadily away from the legacies of the French Revolution. By 1810, the emperor had not only created his new nobility but introduced elaborate court etiquette at his palaces. While he had initially planned his Legion of Honor as a reward for merit in all walks of life, and declared that it should not go primarily to soldiers, in fact some 96 percent of the men wearing its prized decoration came from the military. He had also begun to remake the city of Paris in a distinctly militaristic vein. He expanded the old palace of the Louvre and opened the museum there to display not simply the glories of French art but works looted by his armies from across Europe. A ceremonial arch commemorating his victories went up in its courtyard, and he began work on a much larger one at the end of the Champs Elysées—the Arc de Triomphe. France's artists were mustered to commemorate his endless stream of battles. In place of the revolutionary Bastille Day holiday, he put in place a new national holiday—the "Day of Saint Napoleon," named for an obscure Christian martyr of that name whom the cowed pope had obligingly "discovered." It was celebrated on the emperor's own birthday. Catholicism did not return to its previous place in French life. In fact, Napoleon clashed with the pope and ended up keeping him a prisoner in French territory. But in other ways, Napoleon's subjects might have been forgiven for seeing the First Empire resembling, more and more, the Old Regime.

Meanwhile, the empire was continuing to expand. The need to mobilize ever larger populations to staff and supply the ever more bloated armies, and the logic of the Continental System, fed the unsteady extension of the area under direct imperial control. France annexed the Netherlands, previously ruled by King Louis Bonaparte, along with a chunk of northeastern Spain, part of the north German coastline and the "Illyrian Provinces" of present-day Croatia. But this expansion was a sign of frustration and weakness, not of strength. And even after defeating the Fifth Coalition, Napoleon still had to deal with the ongoing conflict in Spain, many smaller insurgencies in Italy, and various forms of civil strife and disobedience throughout other conquered territories. And the Continental System was springing new holes faster than the French could plug them.

In short, however large and powerful Napoleon's empire looked from outside and however great the conquests it was already trying to digest, it was certain that the wars would continue—indeed, that they would continue on a larger scale than ever. As much as ever, war remained at the heart of Napoleon's rule. His sharpest critic, the Swiss liberal Benjamin Constant, would soon compose an angry pamphlet arguing that in the modern "age of commerce," which had outgrown primitive martial passions, founding a nation on conquest amounted to "a crude and deadly anachronism." But Napoleon could not easily avoid the logic of war. As the year 1812 began, he was already preparing his most ambitious campaign: to invade Russia.

Chapter 5
Downfall, 1812–1815

When Napoleon Bonaparte crossed the Niemen River into Russian territory in June 1812, he brought along some potentially disturbing reading: Voltaire's *History of Charles XII*. It told the story of a king of Sweden, the most admired military leader of his time, who had invaded Russia a century before. But Charles's army, weakened by disease and sheer exhaustion after an eighteen-month trek through hostile territory, came to grief in the decisive battle of Poltava, which proved so disastrous that it sealed Sweden's decline as a military power. Presumably, Napoleon took Voltaire with him in the hope of avoiding Charles's mistakes. At one point, early in the campaign, he told an aide, "We shall not repeat the folly of Charles XII!" But in the end he proved a very bad reader.

Napoleon certainly thought he had good reasons for invading Russia. Tsar Alexander had turned out to be a woefully unreliable ally, defying France's Continental System and flirting with the British. And despite the challenges involved in invading Russia, Napoleon still felt himself unbeatable in land warfare against uniformed enemies. Even with his recent setbacks—especially in Spain—Egypt remained the only one of his major campaigns to have ended squarely in defeat. Indeed, at times the emperor still nurtured fantasies of surpassing Alexander the Great. "I do not fear that long road which is bordered by deserts," an aide remembered him saying. "After all, that long road is the road to

India. Alexander, to reach the Ganges, started from just as distant a point as Moscow."

In fact, it is quite wrong to assume that the Russian campaign was doomed from the start. Despite his fantasies about outdoing Alexander, Napoleon had no desire to annex the vast country to his own empire or to subjugate its population (very much unlike Hitler, 130 years later). He wanted only to smash Russia's army—as he had done once already, so spectacularly, at Austerlitz—in order to compel its political cooperation. And he assembled the most powerful military force yet seen in European history for this purpose. It comprised, altogether, some 655,000 soldiers, including 450,000 in the main army group. It was a genuinely European force, drawing more heavily from allies, and from conquered territories, than from France itself. The soldiers were seasoned and well trained. Some fifty thousand civilians, including many women, accompanied them.

Unfortunately, Napoleon had given the Russians a long time to prepare. As early as 1810 they had foreseen the coming invasion and pondered the most likely means of defeating it. As Russian officer Piotr Chuikevich wrote in a planning memo, the key was "to plan and pursue a war exactly contrary to what the enemy wants." In other words, to avoid the sort of major battle that could destroy the Russian army. Instead, as the tsar himself confided to another general, the goal was "gaining time and drawing out the war as long as possible." If Napoleon came, the Russians would retreat into the depths of their vast country, destroying supplies as they went. And the Russians had competent commanders, including the legendary sixty-six-year-old Mikhail Kutuzov. Despite the fact that a musket ball had passed clean through his head nearly forty years before, leaving him badly scarred and nearly blind, Kutuzov had formidable tactical skills.

Napoleon faced other obstacles. The very size of his army made it harder for him to control and maneuver than the forces he had commanded early in his career. The problems of ruling a huge and troubled empire pressed in on him, distracting him from the campaign. And his health hobbled him more and more. Like Charles XII, who had commanded his forces at Poltava from a stretcher after receiving a leg wound, Napoleon was virtually incapacitated in several battles against the Russians. The weather, finally, posed a variety of problems from the start. Napoleon's Russian campaign is best remembered for the frigid retreat, but the scorching summer advance proved almost as damaging to the Grande Armée. Men wearing thick cloth uniforms and carrying heavy packs had to march hundreds of miles in ninety-degree heat. Supplies of food and drink ran short, forcing them to filter stagnant, worm-infested water through linen. Dysentery followed and turned the road to Moscow into one long, foul-smelling open latrine.

At several moments Napoleon came close to turning his forces around, but each time ended up pushing forward in the hope of catching the Russians. In mid-August, he came close at Smolensk but gained little but the city's smoking ruins. He put a brave face on the Pyrrhic victory, however, saying to his officers: "Gentlemen, remember the words of a Roman emperor. 'A dead enemy always smells sweet.'" Then on September 7 he finally confronted the main Russian force at Borodino, outside Moscow. Shaking with fever and urinary pain, he remained behind the lines and directed his forces with a caution that the younger Napoleon would have scorned, holding back his beloved elite Imperial Guard. The battle itself was a slaughterhouse. The French lost thirty to thirty-five thousand men killed and wounded; the Russians as many as fifty thousand. But Kutuzov managed to keep the remainder of his forces intact and retreated successfully, making Borodino a French victory but not the decisive one Napoleon had hoped for. A week later the French marched into Moscow (which Saint Petersburg had replaced as the capital a century before) to find it largely deserted. Between straggling, disease, and death, Napoleon had already lost more than a third of his men.

Even so, the campaign did not yet look like a disaster. Napoleon had led his men on another epic march—more than six hundred miles. He had won victories on the battlefield and occupied one of his adversary's major cities. Tsar Alexander, a man prone to wild mood swings, fell into a depression. "Served as badly as I have been," he wrote despairingly to his sister, "facing a hellish adversary who…can draw upon all Europe, and upon a mass of men of genius who have been shaped by twenty years of revolutions and war, is it so surprising that I have met with failures?"

But then, on September 14, Napoleon's hopes went up quite literally in smoke when Russian saboteurs carried out orders to burn Moscow. The conflagration, Europe's worst since the Great Fire of London of 1666, destroyed nearly two-thirds of the city's private residences and killed thousands. Napoleon himself later remembered an astonishing spectacle: "a sea and billows of fire, a sky and clouds of flame—mountains of red rolling flames, like immense waves of the sea." The fire left Moscow uninhabitable, forcing the French army to withdraw. And the emperor then made matters much worse by delaying the army's departure for nearly a month, believing his men had plenty of time before winter set in. Instead, one of the coldest winters on record began earlier than usual. On one occasion temperatures fell to lower than thirty-five degrees below zero.

The French retreat from Moscow has deservedly gone down in history as one of the greatest military catastrophes of all time. Napoleon's forces were ill prepared for the murderous cold, all the more so since they had laden their carriages with loot, skimping on warm clothes and food. The survivors would later recount in detail the phantasmagorical horrors they experienced as the Grande Armée plodded through a seemingly endless plain of snow. Frostbite seized appendages; snow glare induced temporary blindness. Each morning the sun rose on the frost-covered corpses of men who had fallen asleep and frozen solid in the night. Horses, dead and living, were devoured raw, while desperate soldiers sought warmth in the animals' eviscerated bellies. Buglers froze where they stood, their instruments still pressed to their lips. It took more than a month for the rapidly shrinking army to reach the Berezina River, where heroic Dutch sappers, standing in the frigid water up to their chins for up to fifteen minutes at a time, constructed makeshift bridges to provide an escape from approaching Russians. When the Russians attacked, one bridge collapsed, and a mad panic ensued on the other. Thousands were trampled or knocked into the swirling waters. All in all, of the original 655,000-strong force, scarcely 85,000 men made it back out of Russia. Some 370,000 had died; 200,000 more were prisoners or missing. Napoleon himself left the army in early December and headed back to Paris. At an inn in Lithuania where he stopped to rest and change clothes, the townspeople grabbed at his used shirt and stockings as if they were holy relics. But whatever odor of sanctity still clung to him in their eyes, in the world at large his aura of invincibility had disappeared.

In the popular imagination, Napoleon's downfall proceeded directly from this catastrophe. Historians caution, however, that the emperor still controlled vast territories and could draw on unmatched human resources. In early 1813 the French government successfully carried out an extraordinary levy of 350,000 men to replace the losses in Russia. The campaigns of 1813, which Napoleon fought in Germany against the so-called Sixth Coalition, included several close-run battles that came close to reversing his fortunes. Napoleon showed no compunction in continuing the struggle and in sacrificing hundreds of thousands more men. "A man like me," he stated frankly in 1813, seeking to convince the Austrian statesman Metternich of his willingness to continue the war, "does not give a shit about the lives of a million men."

Nonetheless, the odds had shifted strongly against him. The Russian winter had claimed not just soldiers but tough, experienced soldiers—Napoleon's Imperial Guard suffered especially high losses—and the raw recruits of 1813 could not easily replace them. The French had also lost close to two hundred thousand horses, twelve hundred artillery pieces, and untold tons of cannon shot, gunpowder, cartridge pouches, flints, uniforms, boots, and saddles. At the battle of Lützen in Germany in May 1813, Napoleon prevailed but could not pursue and destroy the enemy army because he lacked the necessary cavalry. At Leipzig, in October, he ran out of cannon shot.

The Russian disaster, combined with further losses to Wellington in Spain, also spelled doom for Napoleon's Continental System and his hope to defeat Britain by strangling its trade. To the contrary, British economic prospects now looked promising enough that in the summer of 1813 London could provide its continental allies with an outright subsidy of 2 million pounds and a credit of 2 1/2 million more. The money directly supported a Russian army of 160,000 men marching westward.

Just as devastating were the defeat's psychological effects. In France itself the tightly controlled press and boastful military dispatches had sustained the myth of Napoleon's invincibility even after battles like Eylau, and the reverses in Spain. In October 1812, when a dismissed general named Claude-François de Malet attempted a coup d'état in Paris, he took care first to spread the rumor of Napoleon's death. The rumor was quickly disproved, and the coup failed miserably, leading to Malet's quick trial and execution. But in early December 1812, the *Twenty-Ninth Bulletin of the Grande Armée* admitted, for the first time, the dreadful calamity that had struck the French army and spoke frankly about the losses in Russia. The elaborate surveillance system designed by Joseph Fouché began to report strikingly higher levels of anxiety and discontent among the population.

Outside France, meanwhile, the news of the Russian campaign led directly to the splintering of Napoleon's coalition. For years, Prussian officers and officials had chafed at the French alliance into which their humiliating 1806 defeat had forced them. But in the last days of 1812 a thirty-thousand-man Prussian army under General Hans-David Yorck took the unprecedented step of switching sides. "With a bloody heart I rip asunder the bonds of obedience, and wage war on my own account," Yorck declared. Over the next few months, Prussia's King Frederick William grew increasingly concerned that unless he himself followed Yorck's example, he might face the previously unimaginable prospect of a military revolt by an army that had always stood as the paragon of unquestioning obedience to its sovereign. In March 1813 he gave in and declared war on France. Sweden soon followed, despite the fact that its new crown prince, Jean-Baptiste Bernadotte, had been one of Napoleon's marshals. Austria, even with its new family ties to the Bonapartes, wavered as well, adopting a position of neutrality.

A final factor turning the tide against Napoleon involved the allies' increasingly effective military performance. Even before the Russian campaign, they had realized that they could no longer rely on the sort of armies they had deployed before the French Revolution, composed largely of long-serving professionals and commanded by aristocrats. As early as 1808, the Austrian emperor had experimented with a *Landwehr* (home army), in which all adult males from large parts of the empire would serve. The next year, as already mentioned, the supporters of the Bourbon King Fernando authorized all Spanish adult males to carry out attacks on French soldiers swelling the ranks of the guerrillas. In 1813, Prussia's King Frederick William introduced forms of compulsory military service for all adult males, and with explicit reference to the Spanish example called on the population to resist the French by whatever means possible. In addition, the uniformed allied armies increasingly copied Napoleon's reliance on forced marches and shock attacks by concentrations of cavalry and massive infantry columns. This shift not only blunted Napoleon's tactical advantage but led to a further massive increase in the size of battles, just at the moment when the French had suffered such horrific losses.

It is worth asking why, at this point, Napoleon and the allies did not make peace. On the one hand the drastically changed odds had removed any realistic chance that the war could end in a French triumph. On the other, at least through the summer of 1813, the allies had not yet seriously contemplated removing Napoleon from power. The British did, still, technically recognize the self-proclaimed Louis XVIII as the legitimate ruler of France. But two decades after the Revolution, the Bourbons were largely forgotten. Peace negotiations with Napoleon in fact dragged on through much of 1813, with Austria as a mediator. Starting in early June, the two sides even observed a six-week truce. But a settlement failed to materialize.

Chance and personality certainly played a role in this failure, but the reasons lie above all in the nature of the war, and of Napoleon's regime. Despite a readiness to negotiate, the monarchs of Britain, Russia, and Prussia still had trouble recognizing Napoleon, the son of the French Revolution, as a truly legitimate adversary. Indeed, they continued to wage an unprecedented propaganda campaign against him, demonizing him personally with an intensity they had never deployed against established dynastic adversaries. A popular German engraving portrayed him as the son of the Devil, while the German poet Ernst Moritz Arndt actually wrote that in Napoleon, "Satan has come, and taken on flesh and blood." As early as November 1806 the Holy Synod of the Russian Orthodox Church condemned Napoleon as a "precursor of the Antichrist." In September 1812, as Moscow was burning, Tsar Alexander declared: "Napoleon or me, I or him, we cannot both rule at the same time."

Carl von Clausewitz, the Prussian officer and future military strategist, powerfully expressed how war had changed in a text he wrote in 1812, while fighting alongside the Russians. Before the French Revolution, he wrote, "war was waged in the way that a pair of duelists carried out their pedantic struggle." But, he continued, "there is no more talk of this sort of war, and one

Das ist mein lieber Sohn, an dem ich Wohlgefallen habe.

9. In the countries opposed to Napoleon, vicious caricatures of the emperor appeared, including this German engraving portraying him as the son of the Devil. Its caption reads: "This is my dear son, in whom I am well pleased."

would have to be blind, not to be able to perceive the difference with ... the wars that our age and our conditions require.... The war of the present time is a war of all against all. It is not the King who wars on a king, not an army which wars on an army, but a people which wars on another." In Germany, as before in Spain, educated elites perceived the conflict—which Germans still refer to as the "War of Liberation"—as a national one. Poets and artists produced torrents of patriotic anti-French invective; idealistic young men from across German-speaking Europe rushed to serve in Prussian "free corps." Although the extent to which the movement represented a true "German national awakening" has been exaggerated, it became a powerful inspiration for future German nationalists.

Napoleon himself, meanwhile, felt conflicted at the very idea of making a less than triumphant peace. To be sure, at various points of his rule he had happily, if unconvincingly, allowed his own propagandists to portray him as a peaceful soul, forced to take the field only to protect his people against the greed and aggression of unreasonable adversaries. But at heart, he still believed in the point he had clearly stated as early as 1803: the French people would support him only so long as he remained covered in glory. In the spring of 1813 he mused that an "old established government" could accept a "harsh peace." He, however, was "a new man, I need to be more careful of public opinion." A year later he repeated the point: "My domination will not be able to survive from the day I cease...to be feared." Later still, in exile, he told his small entourage: "I myself was the keystone of an edifice totally new, and raised on a slight foundation! Its stability depended on each of my battles!"

Indeed, Napoleon's rule never escaped dependence on the age's new forms of revolutionary war—of total war. And while the achievements of the Consulate had been impressive, precisely by doing so much to restore domestic stability to France, they relieved the desperate longing for order and security that had helped bring Napoleon to power in the first place. Would the French still accept him as an autocratic monarch if he lacked both the sanction of long tradition and the intoxicating odor of unbroken victory? Perhaps wisely, Napoleon did not want to find out. And so, between his own conflicted attitude and his adversaries' inability to accept his legitimacy, the peace negotiations collapsed. In the summer of 1813 Austria, the supposed mediator, joined the anti-French coalition.

The campaigns of 1813 in Germany did see some French successes, and at a few moments Napoleon's old verve and talent showed through on the battlefield. But the losses in Russia of horses, materiel, and experienced men told against him at several decisive moments. He also made his share of strategic mistakes, notably dividing his forces before the mammoth Battle of Leipzig in October and leaving a crucial detachment behind in the Saxon capital of Dresden. Leipzig, also known as the "Battle of the Nations," was the largest battle ever fought in European history up to that time, continuing the previous decade's pattern of exponential expansion. It took place over a three-day period, with the French facing significant contingents from Russia, Prussia, Austria, and Sweden. Five hundred thousand soldiers participated, and well over one hundred thousand were killed and wounded. Chance played a role, especially when a panicky French corporal set off the explosives on a key bridge before the French army had finished crossing it, trapping the French rear guard in the city and turning what was already a defeat into a catastrophe. But even if Napoleon had avoided this particular calamity, he simply did not have the resources to prevail.

Adding to his woes was the collapse of another front. Three months before Leipzig, his brother Joseph, king of Spain, had lost decisively to Lord Wellington at the battle of Vitoria in northern Spain. Joseph himself fled the battlefield in a panic, leaving carriages full of looted Spanish treasures to be looted again by delighted redcoats. Then, just a week and a half before Leipzig, Wellington went on to defeat Marshal Soult at the Bidassoa River, which separated Spain from France, and secured the first allied foothold on pre-1792 French territory since before Napoleon's coronation. So now France was open to invasion from both the south and the east, in what would become Napoleon's endgame.

Napoleon's principal opponents in this endgame made an odd pair. Tsar Alexander, now in his late thirties, was turning increasingly religious, indeed almost mystical, in his beliefs. He was the most feared and despotic ruler in Europe, brooking no domestic opposition while presiding over a system that kept over half his people in virtual slavery as serfs. But he was coming to dream that victory over Napoleon could usher in a new age of harmony and peace. He even briefly toyed with the idea of restoring a moderate republic in France, if doing so would ensure a stable peace settlement. Alexander's unlikely partner was the Austrian foreign minister, Klemens, Count von Metternich, an elegant, vain, handsome, and supremely competent statesman whose "blue-eyed, benevolent gaze would fool God himself," as Stendhal later wrote. Coming into office after Napoleon's 1809 defeat of Austria, until the Russian campaign Metternich pursued a policy of cooperation with France, personally negotiating the emperor's marriage to the Austrian Marie-Louise. Metternich prized, above all, the ideal of a balance of power and feared excessive Russian expansion into central Europe. Even after 1812, he initially tried to make Austria a neutral mediator, and he invested considerable time and energy in the peace negotiations. But when the negotiations collapsed, he committed Austria to the cause of Napoleon's defeat.

Even after the allies entered France in early 1814, Napoleon was determined to keep fighting and at times fought brilliantly. In February he beat the Prussians three times in five days and then marched his weary soldiers forty-seven miles in just thirty-six hours to successfully repel a Russian force. A month later he retook the eastern French city of Reims. But Wellington's men, marching north from the Pyrenees, occupied Bordeaux on March 12 and moved toward Toulouse. Then at Arcis-sur-Aube on March 20–21, overwhelming allied numbers forced Napoleon himself to retreat. The emperor nearly died when a howitzer shell exploded under his horse. He could no longer protect Paris, and on March 31 the allies entered the French capital. Napoleon withdrew to Fontainebleau, forty miles southeast of the city.

On the evening of March 31, Tsar Alexander, accompanied by Prussia's King Frederick William and the Austrian commander-in-chief, Prince Karl Phillip von Schwarzenberg, rode into Paris, cheered by crowds grateful that the city had been spared the fate of Moscow. Their destination was the mansion of Talleyrand, the former bishop, revolutionary, and foreign minister to Napoleon. Despite having left office in 1807, and despite his subsequent banishment for conspiring with the allies, Talleyrand had survived the war in comfort (proof, once again, of Napoleon's relative mildness toward domestic opposition). He had stayed in touch with Metternich, and he retained considerable influence among France's ruling elites. He now did more than anyone else to determine how Napoleon's rule would end.

Tsar Alexander and the other allies had by this point committed themselves to removing Napoleon from power. As the British minister to Austria stated, "so long as he lives, there can be no security." But who would replace him? His three-year-old son, perhaps under the regency of the Austrian-born empress? Some new royal figure? Or the Bourbon pretender, Louis XVIII? As noted, this last solution had seemed remote for many years. But in early March, as the British had advanced toward Bordeaux, a group of young supporters of the exiled dynasty, styling themselves the Chevaliers de la Foi (Knights of the Faith) staged an impressive demonstration in the city. The mayor, an ally of theirs, greeted the British vanguard by tearing off his Napoleonic insignia, donning a sash in the white of the Bourbon dynasty, and declaring his loyalty to King Louis. Over the next weeks, support for the Bourbons grew. Talleyrand felt the exiled family offered France the best chance of receiving a fair deal from the British, who would have a harder time taking advantage of a king they had long recognized, if only in name, as the country's legitimate sovereign. (Talleyrand also thought, needless to say, that Louis best served Talleyrand.) Now, with the tsar and other allied luminaries as his houseguests, Talleyrand pressed for the Bourbon solution. He also, without any authority, called on Napoleon's tame Senate to vote the abolition of the Empire. Motivated largely by fearful self-interest, a majority of the senators present in Paris complied and decreed the establishment of a new provisional government that included Talleyrand himself. There is some credible evidence that Talleyrand schemed to have Napoleon assassinated to guard against his possible return to power, but nothing came of the plot.

Napoleon, at Fontainebleau with tens of thousands of troops still loyal to him, remained defiant. He accepted that he could not continue as emperor and indicated his willingness to abdicate, but only in favor of his son. As long as the army continued to support him he had a chance of success, for the tsar in particular did not want to risk further bloodshed for the sake of the corpulent, uninspiring Louis XVIII—who, hobbled by gout, had not yet even left London. But then several of the army's marshals declared they would no longer fight for Napoleon. And on April 5, even as the allies seemed on the point of agreeing to allow the Bonaparte dynasty to continue, Marshal Auguste Marmont's army corps defected to the allies. Napoleon now had no choice but to abdicate unconditionally. A few days later, seized by despair, he tried to kill himself by swallowing a sachet of poison he had carried with him since the Russian campaign. But the drugs had lost their potency and succeeded only in making him violently ill.

On April 20, Napoleon bade farewell to the men of his Old Guard at Fontainebleau. The scene showed that he had lost none of his sense of theatricality or his instinct for effective publicity. Dressed in his familiar uniform, with his two-pointed hat on his head, he delivered a short speech:

> Soldiers of my Old Guard, I have come to bid you farewell. For twenty years you have accompanied me faithfully on the paths of honor and glory....With men like you, our cause was lost, but the war would have dragged on interminably, and it would have been a civil war....So I am sacrificing our interests to those of our

country.... Do not lament my fate; if I have agreed to live on, it is
to serve our glory. I wish to write the history of the great deeds
we have done together. Farewell, my children!

A small convoy of carriages then took him away from
Fontainebleau and south toward the Mediterranean. On May 4
he arrived on the small Italian island of Elba, within sight of his
native Corsica: his new home. The British press joked that
Napoleon could now enjoy some "Elba room." The former master
of total war had finally become its victim.

Yet he had one act still to perform—his most remarkable of all,
the "Hundred Days." Less than a year after leaving France,
Napoleon would return in secret, rally his supporters, and seize
power for a second time. He would restore the Empire, resuscitate
the Grande Armée, and march across the frontier to confront his
enemies. Only after his defeat at Waterloo in June 1815 by
Wellington would his fall from power become permanent.

Few events in European history generated as much shock as
Napoleon's return to power, yet it was not, in fact, entirely
surprising. The settlement of 1814 was riven by two deep tensions,
which opened the door for his dramatic coup. The first concerned
Napoleon himself and the allies' inability to decide whether to
treat him as a defeated monarch or a criminal in custody. Long
political tradition made it difficult for them not to recognize the
sovereign attributes of a ruler they had negotiated with—indeed,
in many cases, allied with—and who had married into the
Habsburg dynasty. So even as the white flag of the Bourbons
rose over French cities and towns, the allies gave Napoleon the
trappings of sovereignty on Elba, including a small military
entourage, a flag, and the title "emperor." Yet the British navy
remained in control of the island and denied Napoleon permission
to come and go as he pleased. Nor did the allies allow him the
company of his wife, whose father, the Austrian emperor, had
pressured her to return to Vienna along with Napoleon's young

heir. Could this contradictory situation endure? The allies
themselves were not sure, and as early as December 1814, rumors
reached Elba that they might soon move Napoleon elsewhere.

The other tension involved the Bourbon Restoration in France.
Despite the hopes of a few diehards, a return to the Old Regime,
with its estates and aristocrats and powerful Catholic Church, was
impossible. Far too much had changed since 1789, including the
introduction of civic equality and the large-scale transfer of land
from the Church and noble émigrés, in large part, to the peasantry.
Louis XVIII, who finally returned to Paris in May, understood this
point. In most respects he possessed relatively liberal inclinations,
and sought—very much like Napoleon, in fact—to reconcile the
Old Regime and the Revolution in his own person. He and his
advisors envisaged a regime that would preserve most of the
administrative reforms of the Revolution and the Consulate.

The king would share power with an elected parliament—albeit
one elected by a small minority of wealthy men. Had Louis
submitted his new constitution to a plebiscite, as Napoleon
had done, he might well have established his rule on a firm basis.
But on this very point—popular sovereignty—he refused to make
concessions. He was the chosen of God, and rather than accepting
the constitution *from* the people, he insisted on "granting" it *to*
them, while banishing the tricolor flag for which so many of them
had died. His government also signed with the allies the Treaty of
Paris, which, while refraining from drastic sanctions on France,
reduced it to its 1792 borders. Discontent quickly grew, along with
fears that the Bourbons might yet take measures to return
property to the Church and émigrés. And with no credible
liberal party on the scene, the discontent quickly translated into
renewed enthusiasm for the man who had so famously identified
himself with the Revolution: Napoleon.

It was under these conditions that Napoleon fled Elba on
February 26, 1815, easily evading lackluster British and French

patrols and landing on the French coast three days later. As he marched north to Paris, he met with an increasingly enthusiastic response from stunned onlookers, and his talent for stage-managing dramatic events for maximum effect, as in the March 7 "encounter at Laffrey," had not deserted him. More such events followed. His longtime subordinate Marshal Michel Ney had sworn an oath of loyalty to Louis XVIII, and on hearing of Napoleon's return promised to bring the emperor to Paris in an iron cage. On March 14 Ney changed sides again and tearfully embraced his old master. Five days later, the army defending Paris declared its loyalty to Napoleon as well. Louis XVIII, who had pledged to die rather than abandon his capital, abandoned his capital and fled the country. On March 20, tens of thousands of Parisians, many of them weeping hysterically with joy, welcomed Napoleon back to the city.

The so-called flight of the eagle had been unmatchable as drama. But having flown, what would the eagle do next? With France still weakened from years of war, its armies diminished, and its frontiers contracted, Napoleon had no hope of restoring an autocracy grounded in conquest and glory. To win acceptance as France's legitimate sovereign, he needed the population's support as expressed through peaceful democratic means, and this meant, inescapably, identifying himself more firmly than ever with the Revolution. Even before reaching Paris he issued decrees reinstating the tricolor flag and taking measures against the noble émigrés who had returned to France in the past year. Once back in power, he invited his liberal critic Benjamin Constant to compose an "Additional Act" to complement his imperial constitution. Constant, despite having recently compared Napoleon to Attila and Genghis Khan, could not resist the temptation. The document he wrote formally recognized the sovereignty of the French nation and made provisions for limited press freedom and judicial independence. A new legislature would include an elected lower chamber, although with the suffrage still restricted to men of property. As before, Napoleon called for a plebiscite to approve the modified constitution, and while only a fifth of the eligible voters turned out, the evidence suggests that he won an authentic majority. On June 1, dressed in a luxurious and ill-tailored Roman costume in which he could barely move, Napoleon presided over a mammoth festival in Paris to celebrate the foundation of his newest regime.

The allies, however, had different ideas. Their representatives had been meeting since September in an unprecedented gathering, the Congress of Vienna, to plan the future of the continent. It would eventually produce one of the longest lasting and effective peace settlements in European history, based on a system whereby the great powers would cooperate to manage crises and avoid full-scale war. France, represented by the skillful Talleyrand, played an increasingly important role, notably when tensions arose between the Russians and other allies. The "flight of the eagle" generated as much shock in Vienna as in Paris, but in at least one sense it clarified matters greatly. Was Napoleon a sovereign adversary or an outlaw? Hearing the news from France, the deputies immediately declared that by his actions, Napoleon "has shown in the face of the world that there can be neither peace nor truce with him... Napoleon Bonaparte is... an Enemy and Disturber of the tranquility of the World." They quickly formed yet another anti-French coalition (the seventh) and planned a new campaign.

Napoleon himself knew that the odds were strongly against him. Although frantically building up his military forces through renewed conscription and a virtual nationalization of armaments production, he could not wait for the far more powerful allied armies to descend on him. His only hope was to deal them a quick and devastating blow to force them to come to terms. In June, at the head of 124,000 men, he moved to attack the British and Prussians in Belgium, which the allies had stripped from France and annexed to the Kingdom of Holland. On June 16 at Ligny he defeated the Prussians, although not decisively. Six miles away,

Marshal Ney fought the British to a draw at Quatre-Bras. The stage was now set for the decisive battle, two days later, at Waterloo.

Waterloo itself immediately achieved legendary status as one of the greatest battles in history, but in truth it is hard to believe that a French victory there could have actually changed history. The forces deployed against France were simply too great, and the allies too determined. The battle's reputation derives rather from the story told by the British about how their heroic pluck and resolve (forged on the playing fields of Eton!) saved the day, and from the grandeur the French found in heroic, sacrificial defeat. As Victor Hugo, no admirer of Napoleon, would later write:

> In the blink of an eye,
> Just as a piece of burning straw flies up into the wind
> There vanished that sound that had been the Grande Armée,
> And this plain, alas, where today we dream,
> Saw flee those men before whom the universe itself had fled.

The battle itself was a bloodbath, with the highest casualty rate of the entire Napoleonic period (45 percent of all combatants killed or wounded). The British blocked the French advance for much of the day, while intense fighting swirled around two farmhouses. The leadership of Wellington, who had never before confronted Napoleon on the battlefield, proved fundamental, especially in a climactic duel between Napoleon's Old Guard and British redcoats who had taken shelter on the far slope of a hill only to rise up and spray a series of murderous volleys at the key moment. A durable legend holds that Pierre Cambronne, major of the Old Guard, declared that "the Guard dies; it never surrenders." (According to another legend, he simply said "shit.") But the Old Guard, a pale shadow of its pre-Russian self, broke and fled. Just as important as this moment, however, was the timely arrival of vital Prussian reinforcements under the venerable Gebhard von Blücher, and the failure of Napoleon's subordinate Marshal

Emmanuel de Grouchy to bring his troops to the battlefield at the crucial moment.

With the battle lost, Napoleon made little effort to rally his remaining forces but rushed back toward Paris in a vain attempt to keep control of events there. But his new regime, fragile enough to start with, was already tottering, and any attempt to resist the allies further would probably have led to civil war. Napoleon declined this option, again attempted unsuccessfully to pass the throne to his son, and finally abdicated unconditionally for a second time, issuing a lachrymose "Declaration to the French People" in which he announced he was sacrificing himself for the good of the *patrie*. He then made his way to the Atlantic coast in the hope of escaping to the United States. But at the port of Rochefort he found a British squadron waiting for him, and on July 15 he surrendered to Captain Frederick Maitland of HMS *Bellerophon*. The next day the ship bore him away from France for the last time.

Epilogue: 1815–the present

When the *Bellerophon* weighed anchor in Rochefort harbor in July 1815, Napoleon still had six years to live. But unlike the rest of his adult life, these years were ones of inaction and largely of immobility, passed in frustrated exile on the small tropical island of Saint Helena. Napoleon spent these years seeking control not over Europe but over how history would remember him. It was the last chapter of his life but, more important, the first chapter of the longer, hugely contentious story of his historical significance.

Unlike in 1814, there was now no doubt about Napoleon's status in defeat. He was a prisoner, and after keeping him briefly on board ship off Plymouth, the British transported him to the South Atlantic. There he lived under permanent guard, joined by a handful of devoted followers who spent much of their time jotting down his every passing remark for posterity. Napoleon himself took long hours to dictate a rambling and incomplete set of formal reminiscences to one of them, Count Emmanuel de Las Cases. The principal British officer overseeing his confinement for most of his time on the island, Hudson Lowe, subjected him to petty humiliations, such as depriving him of firewood and addressing him only as "General," outraging the entourage and leading to an occasional stir in the European press. Despite many rumors and the occasional plot, rescue efforts never seriously materialized. In 1820 Napoleon fell seriously ill, probably with the stomach cancer that killed his father, although eager conspiracy theorists have suspected poison. On May 5, 1821, he died. He was just fifty-one.

His legacy continued, however, to shape European history in a massive and direct manner for decades. The "Concert of Europe" designed at Vienna by the allies, still reeling from two decades of intense Napoleonic conflict, succeeded in keeping a closely managed peace for longer than any previous European settlement and most subsequent ones as well (far better than Versailles, a century later). But with the allies worried, above all, about renewed outbreaks of revolutionary politics, this peace was also a deeply conservative one, in which the powers (including Restoration France) did not hesitate to crush budding democratic movements with force. In 1823, just nine years after leaving Spain, French soldiers returned there, but this time in the service of the Concert of Europe to help King Fernando suppress liberal opponents. Throughout Europe, the 1820s and 1830s were decades of reaction.

Yet at the same time, Bonapartism as a political model continued to have resonance worldwide. In December 1804, one onlooker at Napoleon's coronation had been an impressionable twenty-one year-old Venezuelan named Simon Bolívar. "The universal acclaim and the interest which his person inspired," Bolívar later remembered, "made me think of the slavery of my country, and the glory that would benefit the one who liberated it." Throughout his own long career as liberator and authoritarian ruler in South America, Bolívar took explicit inspiration from Napoleon, as did many future caudillos. In the Americas, the figure of the glorious general who took power to redeem and purify his county long remained a potent one. Latin American countries also copied many of Napoleon's administrative reforms and adopted versions of his civil code. Even in Europe, the reforms and laws instituted under Napoleonic rule, especially in Germany and Italy, survived Napoleon himself. In Prussia, the drastic reforms enacted in response to the catastrophic defeat of 1806 at Napoleon's hands helped to shape the state that would dominate and unite Germany in the nineteenth century.

Napoleon also remained a figure of obsession for professional soldiers. Everywhere in the world they studied his campaigns in detail, seeking to extract the key to future victories. Carl von Clausewitz, who fought against France in 1812, hated Napoleon but believed that he had provided the model for the "absolute warfare" that the Prussian described in his classic book of strategy, *On War*. The American general George McClellan, despite displaying a most un-Napoleonic caution on the battlefields of the Civil War, exulted in the nickname of the "Young Napoleon." French and German strategists of the late nineteenth century took inspiration from Napoleon in developing new tactical doctrines centered on massive, sacrificial infantry offensives—doctrines that led directly to the slaughterhouse of the World War I trenches.

The Napoleonic wars left France itself exhausted and exsanguinated, and the allies did not help matters by imposing significantly harsher terms in 1815 than a year earlier. The effects of the long British blockade gravely damaged the flourishing Atlantic trade that France had enjoyed before the Revolution and, by destroying so much French capital, delayed its industrialization. Economically, to a certain extent France turned inward on itself. If its population remained considerably more agricultural than its northern neighbors until well into the twentieth century, the reason lies partly with Napoleon.

Politically, the years of Napoleonic rule ended up doing nothing to heal the political divide that had opened up in France with the Revolution. "We believe we are one nation," the historian Augustin Thierry could write in 1820, "but we are actually two nations on the same soil, two nations at war in their memories and irreconcilable in their hopes for the future." Louis XVIII, returning to France for the second time after Waterloo (French wits called him "Louis deux fois neuf"), found it painfully difficult

111

to control the reactionaries in his own camp, who now more than ever dreamed of restoring the Old Regime. His younger brother and successor, who came to the throne in 1824 as Charles X, moved things in an even more reactionary direction, eventually provoking the Revolution of 1830. That event brought to power a more moderate king, Louis-Philippe, but he too ultimately found it impossible to reconcile the warring parties and rule from the center. Deep ideological divides continued to plague French politics through the nineteenth century and into the first half of the twentieth.

Napoleon himself, thanks especially to his forced move to the left during the Hundred Days, remained closely associated with the Revolution throughout the decades that followed Waterloo. The nervous police forces of the Restoration kept close watch on his sympathizers, convinced that the country was on the verge of a joint Jacobin-Bonapartist uprising. Surviving Bonapartists themselves indeed plotted, albeit for the most part ineffectually, and did what they could to keep faith with the emperor, wearing violets in their lapels as a sign of their devotion. (Like Napoleon, the flowers returned in the early spring.)

The Napoleonic legend received an enormous boost in France and elsewhere when the emperor's companion in exile, Emmanuel de Las Cases, published his *Memorial of Saint Helena* in 1822. A long, disjointed book, it mixed Las Cases's account of the exile itself with lengthy transcriptions of Napoleon's reminiscences, in a manner that today has an almost postmodern feel. The lengthy recital of the emperor's petty struggles to receive due marks of respect from Hudson Lowe and the description of his fallen circumstances, juxtaposed with Napoleon's own recollections of his greatest triumphs, gave the book extraordinary pathos and made it one of the century's greatest literary sensations. "What a novel my life has been," the book recorded Napoleon as saying, and in Las Cases's hands, the life indeed became literature. In Stendhal's *The Red and the Black*, the young hero, Julien Sorel, nothing if not Napoleonic in his ambition, is first introduced mourning over a copy of *The Memorial of Saint Helena* that his brutish father has knocked into a stream.

During the following decades, the heyday of European Romanticism, Napoleon would occupy a central place in European literature and art. His youth at the time of his greatest triumphs and the elemental forces that seemed to surge within him made him the perfect Romantic hero. Even in the hands of as strictly classical a painter as David, his irresistible motion, and flowing hair, had seemed to anticipate later Romantic effusions. The celebration of his person and his exploits became all the more irresistible to the Romantics as the years passed, as the memory of wartime suffering receded and the contrast grew seemingly ever greater between his passions and glory and the dull, crabbed texture of daily life in an increasingly avaricious postwar Europe. The greatest of French Romantic authors, Victor Hugo, the son of a Napoleonic general, wrestled with Napoleon's ghost all his life, lamenting the political tyranny and the human suffering but always hailing the "sublime spectacle." Hugo returned to episodes of Napoleon's career endlessly in his work, notably including a brilliant account of Waterloo in *Les Misérables*. His single most famous poem, "The Expiation," tells the story of the emperor's fall, from Russia to Waterloo, Saint Helena, and even beyond, into the tomb. In that corner of the patriotic imagination where the British long kept "The Charge of the Light Brigade," and Americans "The Midnight Ride of Paul Revere," the French kept "The Expiation." Many elderly French people can still recite long passages from memory.

In 1840, France's King Louis-Philippe, eager to shore up his own sagging fortunes, agreed to have Napoleon's remains brought back to France from Saint Helena and reburied. The so-called *retour des cendres* (return of the remains) became the occasion for an outpouring of emotion that almost matched the "flight of the eagle." Weeping veterans of the Grande Armée lined the boulevards as the funerary procession made its way toward the Hôtel des Invalides in Paris. There Napoleon was entombed in a massive sarcophagus of red porphyry, cut in the shape of a great wave. It is over-the-top in suitably Napoleonic fashion. In subsequent years, Napoleon remained as ubiquitous as ever in French culture. Through at least the 1850s, more madmen in France claimed his identity than any other. (A few madwomen did too.)

His continuing popularity helps explain how one of the least competent political adventurers in European history nonetheless managed to become one of France's longest lasting rulers in the mid-nineteenth century. Louis-Napoleon Bonaparte, the son of Napoleon's younger brother Louis, had his uncle's ambition but little of his charisma and none of his genius. In 1836 and then again in 1840 he made farcical attempts to stage a coup d'état in

10. In 1840, Napoleon's body was brought back from Saint Helena to rest in this magnificent tomb of porphyry stone in Les Invalides, in Paris.

France, failing miserably on each occasion and ending up in prison for six years after the second. But in 1848 yet another French Revolution toppled King Louis-Philippe and replaced his reign with the unstable Second Republic. Amid fears of civil war, Louis-Napoleon won election as president and after three years of frustrating political conflict seized dictatorial power by force.

In 1852 he proclaimed himself Emperor Napoleon III. ("Napoleon II," the son of Marie-Louise, had died without issue, of tuberculosis, at age twenty-one.) The "Second Empire" lasted until Napoleon III fell from power after unwisely going to war with Prussia in 1870. Only with his fall did Bonapartism as an organized political force finally disappear from France. Even then, for another century the image of the glorious general as savior figure continued to have an important place in French politics. Charles de Gaulle was Napoleon's heir in more ways than one.

In the twentieth and twenty-first centuries, Napoleon ceased to have the same direct, living presence in Western politics and culture, but he has been anything but forgotten. In France, the laws and institutions he created still largely stand, and so do their copies in many other states. Much of central Paris still bears his mark, from the additions to the Louvre to the Arc de Triomphe, the church of the Madeleine, and the victory column in the Place Vendôme. Tourists still troop in reverently to look at his sarcophagus. A chilling photograph from June 1940 shows Adolf Hitler staring down at it, pensively. Film, television, and literature have returned to Napoleon at regular intervals. Abel Gance's grandiose 1927 silent film *Napoleon*, about his early life, stands as a landmark in film history, notably through innovative technical features such as multiscreen projection. French and American television miniseries about Napoleon, generally of execrable quality, continue to appear at regular intervals. The French novelist Patrick Rambaud has published an excellent trilogy of novels, highly critical of the emperor, that follow the ordinary soldiers who suffered in his wake. Simon Leys's novella *The Death of Napoleon* amusingly imagines the emperor escaping from his British captors after Waterloo and making his way back to Paris, where he proves unable to convince anyone of his true identity. At one point he visits an insane asylum and comes face to face with several self-proclaimed Napoleons, all of who seem more Napoleonic than he does.

All the same, his name no longer functions as either a political rallying cry or an artistic symbol. His image is most often deployed not to evoke ineffable glory but for a laugh or to sell a product. It appears in advertisements for everything from cognac to cigars to stereo systems. One poster from the late twentieth century showed a well-known posthumous portrait with Napoleon's hand in its familiar position stuck inside his vest. "Some say it was merely a pose," reads the caption. "We think it was heartburn."

Because of his son's early death, Napoleon does not have any legitimate descendants who might today keep alive some thin flame of devotion to his memory. He does have numerous illegitimate descendants, however. His Polish mistress, Maria Walewska, gave him a son known as Alexandre Colonna-Walewski, who bore a striking resemblance to him and became foreign minister for five years to Napoleon III. Alexandre had a son by the Jewish actress Rachel Félix, giving Napoleon a long line of Jewish descendants.

But for more than a century, the group most systematically concerned with Napoleon has been, inevitably, the historical profession. To historians he remains a source of endless fascination—and since the history-reading public retains an insatiable appetite for books on the subject, a reliable source of income as well. In one single twenty-year period, more than a dozen full-scale biographies appeared in the English language alone. Starting in the mid-1990s, bicentennial conferences and celebrations tracked Napoleon's career, at a two-hundred-year remove, in minute detail. ("Where did we meet?" an eminent Napoleonic historian once asked me. "Was it at the Marengo conference? No, the Austerlitz conference, surely...") In 2015, alas, this traveling Napoleon roadshow finally met its Waterloo.

Historians have had an odd relationship with Napoleon, though. Throughout the nineteenth and early twentieth centuries they mostly fell, all too simplistically, into two camps: supporters and opponents. The Dutch historian Pieter Geyl, surveying their arguments, even published a book in 1946 entitled *Napoleon For and Against*. Despite uncovering great masses of source material, most of the historical works generally spent too much time refighting old battles to provide much genuine illumination. The pressure to take a side did eventually diminish, but just at that moment, even if the sheer volume of work on Napoleonic subjects remained constant, cutting-edge historical research began to neglect or even ignore him altogether. Military history was falling out of favor in most leading Western universities. The most exciting new historical work looked to the experiences of ordinary people and especially to oppressed groups, such as women and racial and sexual minorities. The long-influential Marxist school put more emphasis on the "bourgeois revolution" of 1789, which they thought Napoleon had continued, and on the Industrial Revolution. The *American Historical Review*, the flagship journal of the historical profession in the United States, went more than thirty-five years without devoting a single substantive article to him.

In the early twenty-first century the situation has again begun to change. Younger historians have worked to reintegrate warfare into studies of Western politics and society, using techniques drawn from anthropology and even literary studies to investigate what they term the "culture of war." A revival of interest in biography as a historical genre has inevitably directed renewed attention to one of the most important and best documented Western lives. And a new attention to global patterns of movement, trade, and domination has put the spotlight on the phenomenon of imperialism, including Napoleon's important if short-lived venture in empire-building. (The historian Michael Broers has examined Napoleon's policies in Italy as an example of "cultural imperialism.")

Much of this new work has, perhaps inevitably, treated Napoleon very harshly, sometimes to the point of reviving the sort of moralistic condemnations surveyed by Geyl. Following the lead of the literary critic Edward Said, historians have criticized Napoleon's Egyptian expedition not just as the first act of modern European imperialism but as the starting point for a current of "orientalist" thought that justified imperialism by casting "eastern" societies as uniformly weak, effete, and irrational. Napoleon has come in for even sharper condemnation for his cynical treatment of France's Caribbean colonies and especially for his reestablishment of slavery there in 1802, reversing the emancipation decree of the revolutionary National Convention. The French author Claude Ribbe, in 2005, went so far as to accuse Napoleon of planning genocide against Caribbean blacks. A former prime minister, the Socialist Lionel Jospin, added to the chorus in 2014 with *Le mal napoléonien*, which can be translated as "The Napoleonic Evil." He flayed Napoleon not only for reestablishing slavery but for betraying the French Revolution, creating a "despotic police-state regime," repressing women, and sacrificing millions of lives and France's national interest for the sake of personal ambition. Even Patrice Gueniffey, one of the most important French biographers, while still praising Napoleon for his institution-building and for his role in securing at least part of the legacy of the French Revolution, does so in careful, highly nuanced language.

These historical shifts have had public resonance. Although the French Republic marked the bicentennial of the French Revolution in 1989 with extravagant, enthusiastic celebrations, it has let the many Napoleonic bicentennials pass by largely in official silence. In December 2005, President Jacques Chirac pointedly failed to attend the small-scale ceremony marking the two hundredth anniversary of the Battle of Austerlitz, perhaps the greatest French military victory of all time. The principal monuments to Napoleon in France are the ones he himself erected, and the French Republic is not about to build new ones.

In a basic sense, it is hard not to endorse these criticisms of Napoleon. The man who boasted to Metternich of his indifference to millions of lives is hard indeed to admire. The reestablishment of slavery, the endless slaughter of the battlefields, the authoritarian rule, the imperial ventures, all make for a damning and lengthy indictment. The more favorable biographers have to show how the situation Napoleon inherited from the revolutionary wars placed heavy constraints on his actions—notably by forcing him into the Continental System and everything that followed from it. But the defense, while well argued, ultimately rings false. Of course Napoleon, like everyone, operated under constraints. But if Napoleon did not have free will, who did? If we are to hold any historical figures at all accountable for their actions, surely we must start with the very small number of men who have held the sort of extraordinary power Napoleon wielded in his heyday.

But history, in the end, is not a judicial procedure. It is a quest for understanding. And it is also a quest to expose the full, amazingly broad and varied canvas of human activity. And from this point of view, as Victor Hugo recognized very well, the "sublime spectacle" matters. Napoleon may have been, from many points of view, a criminal, but he was not a criminal on the scale of the twentieth-century dictators, who made mass murder and terror the basis of their social and political systems. For all his crimes and errors, his life also incarnated a sense of sheer human possibility that quite rightly fascinated onlookers at the time and has continued to do so ever since. We look at his life and recoil from parts of it in horror. But at the same time, inescapably, there is something that takes the breath away. As Shakespeare's Cassius said of Caesar, "Why, man, he doth bestride the narrow world / Like a Colossus." What a novel his life was.

References

Preface

Description of the encounter at Laffrey is taken from Henry Houssaye, *1815: La première restauration, le retour de l'île d'Elbe, les cent jours* (Paris: Perrin, 1894), 242–44.

"Sovereign power resides..." appears in *The Old Regime and the French Revolution,* ed. Keith Michael Baker (Chicago: University of Chicago Press, 1987), 49.

"In every part of the state..." quoted in William H. Sewell, Jr., *Work and Revolution in France: The Language of Labor from the Old Regime to 1848* (Cambridge: Cambridge University Press, 1980), 76.

"No longer is it nations..." appears in Jean-Paul Rabaut de Saint-Étienne, *Précis historique de la Révolution française*, 2 vols. (Brussels: Wahlen, 1818), 1: 127.

"Its style of war..." appears in Jacques-Antoine-Hippolyte de Guibert, *Essai général de Tactique, précédé d'un discours sur l'état actuel de la politique et de la science militaire en Europe* (London, 1772), 149.

"The young men will fight..." appears in *Archives parlementaires de 1787 à 1860, Recueil complet des débats législatifs et politiques des Chambres françaises, première série (1787-1799),* ed. M. J. Mavidal and M. E. Laurent, 82 vols. (Paris: Paul Dupont, 1879–1913), 72: 674.

"A war of purification..." appears in Charles-Philippe Ronsin, *La ligue des fanatiques et des tyrans* (Paris: Guillaume junior, 1791), title page.

Chapter 1: The Corsican, 1769–1796

David Hume quoted in Peter Sahlins, *Boundaries: The Making of France and Spain in the Pyrenees* (Berkeley: University of California Press, 1989), 113.

"I lived like a bear..." appears in Napoleon Bonaparte, *Napoléon inconnu: Papiers inédits (1786–1793)*, ed. Frédéric Masson and Guido Biagi, 2 vols. (Paris: Ollendorff, 1895), 2: 202n.

"He drew her hand..." appears in Napoleon Bonaparte, *Oeuvres littéraires et écrits militaires*, ed. Jean Tulard, 3 vols. (Paris: Claude Tchou, 2001), 1: 210.

"Ambition, like all disordered passions," appears in Bonaparte, *Oeuvres littéraires*, 2: 227.

Lucien Bonaparte letter appears in *Napoléon inconnu*, 2: 397.

"In an instant..." quoted in Steven Englund, *Napoleon: A Political Life* (New York: Scribner, 2004), 41.

"I was born," appears in *Correspondance générale de Napoléon*, ed. Thierry Lentz et al., 15 vols. (Paris: Fayard, 2004–), 1: 96.

"The absolute necessity," quoted in Englund, *Napoleon*, 73.

"I draw from your lips," appears in *Correspondance générale*, 1: 285.

Carl von Clausewitz's reflections appear in *On War*, ed. and trans. Michael Howard and Peter Paret (Princeton, NJ: Princeton University Press, 1976), 591.

Chapter 2: The general, 1796–1799

"The man in the street," appears in Ralph Waldo Emerson, *Representative Men* (Boston: Houghton Mifflin, 1903), 225.

"I can't express..." quoted in Philippe Roger, "Mars au Parnasse," in Jean-Claude Bonnet, ed., *L'Empire des muses: Napoléon, les arts et les lettres* (Paris: Belin, 2004), 384.

"The fatherland has the right..." appears in Napoleon Bonaparte, *Correspondance de Napoléon 1er, publiée par ordre de l'empereur Napoléon III*, 32 vols. (Paris: Imprimerie Impériale, 1858–60), 1: 219.

"I will lead you..." quoted in Alan Schom, *Napoleon Bonaparte: A Life* (New York: HarperCollins, 1997), 42.

"Today, glory has written..." appears in *Courrier de l'armée d'Italie* 48 (October 23, 1797): 206.

"We saw them die," appears in *Copies of Original Letters from the Army of General Bonaparte in Egypt* (London: J. Wright, 1798), 143–44.

"Kings bow down," appears in "Ode arabe sur la Conquête de l'Egypte," in *Décade egyptienne* 1 (1798): 86.

"We Frenchmen... are no longer the infidels..." quoted in J. M. Thompson, *Napoleon Bonaparte* (Oxford: Blackwell, 1988), 120 (emphasis added).

"In Egypt I found myself..." quoted in David Chandler, *The Campaigns of Napoleon: The Mind and Method of History's Greatest Soldier* (New York: Scribner's, 1966), 248.

Chapter 3: The First Consul, 1799–1804

"There is a government..." quoted in Thierry Lentz, *Nouvelle histoire du Premier Empire: La France et l'Europe de Napoléon, 1804–1814* (Paris: Fayard, 2007), 224.

Alexis de Tocqueville, *Democracy in America*, trans. Arthur Goldhammer, 2 vols. (New York: Library of America, 2004), 2: 818.

John Adams quoted in Donald R. Kelley, *The Beginning of Ideology: Consciousness and Society in the French Reformation* (Cambridge: Cambridge University Press, 1981), 3.

"Of 500 mayors..." quoted in Isser Woloch, *The New Regime: Transformations of the French Civic Order, 1789–1820s* (New York: Norton, 1994), 123.

Balzac quoted in Englund, *Napoleon*, 196.

"An excellent public spirit..." quoted in Isser Woloch, "The Napoleonic Regime and French Society," in Philip G. Dwyer, ed., *Napoleon and Europe* (London: Routledge, 2001), 61.

"What other glory..." quoted in Englund, *Napoleon*, 231.

Chapter 4: The emperor, 1804–1812

"We need a European law code..." quoted in Pierre-Joseph Proudhon, *Commentaires sur les mémoires de Fouché* (Paris: Paul Ollendorff, 1900), 216.

"Include in your calculations..." appears in Napoleon Bonaparte to Joseph Bonaparte, March 2, 1806, in *Correspondance de Napoléon 1er, publiée par ordre de l'empereur Napoléon III*, 32 vols. (Paris: Imprimerie Impériale, 1858–60), 12: 147.

"To return, after so many years..." appears in *Correspondance de Napoléon*, 13: 680.

French military governor of Navarre quoted in David A. Bell, *The First Total War: Napoleon's Europe and the Birth of Warfare As We Know It* (Boston: Houghton Mifflin, 2007), 286.

Chapter 5: Downfall, 1812–1815

"I do not fear that long road…" quoted in Christopher Herold, *The Mind of Napoleon: A Selection from His Written and Spoken Words* (New York: Columbia University Press, 1955), 199.

Tsar Alexander quoted in Marie-Pierre Rey, *L'effroyable tragédie: Une nouvelle histoire de la campagne de Russie* (Paris: Flammarion, 2012), 194.

"A sea and billows of fire…" quoted in Herold, *Mind of Napoleon*, 205.

Carl von Clausewitz's reflections appear in "Bekenntnisdenkschrift," in *Schriften—Aufsätze—Studien—Briefe*, ed. Werner Hahlweg, 2 vols. (Göttingen: Vandenhoek and Ruprecht, 1966), 1: 749–50.

"Soldiers of my Old Guard…" appears in Agathon-Jean-François Fain, *Manuscrit de 1814* (Paris: Bossange Frères, 1825), 406.

Epilogue: 1815–the present

Bolivar quoted in Lawrence A. Clayton and Michael L. Conniff, *A History of Modern Latin America* (Independence, KY: Cengage, 2004), 28.

"We believe we are one nation…" appears in Augustin Thierry, *Dix ans d'études historiques* (Paris: Furne, 1851), 237.

Further reading

In the academic world, Napoleon Bonaparte is not even a cottage industry—he is heavy industry. Books and articles about him proliferate at an astonishing rate, and the number of serious items devoted to the man rose into the tens of thousands many years ago. Compiling a full bibliography of Napoleoniana would be a Sisyphean task. The most extensive and serious critical bibliography currently available is Philip Dwyer's contribution to the Military History section of Oxford Bibliographies online, which can be found at http://www.oxfordbibliographies.com/view/document/obo-9780199791279/obo-9780199791279-0095.xml. Readers are encouraged to consult it. What follows is a more abbreviated selection of some of the most important current items, with an emphasis on what is available in English.

Biographies

Of the large crop of English-language biographies to have appeared in the twenty-first century, two of the best are Alan Forrest's *Napoleon* (London: Quercus, 2011), and Michael Broers's *Napoleon: Soldier of Destiny* (London: Faber and Faber, 2014, one volume to date). Steven Englund's *Napoleon: A Political Life* (New York: Scribner, 2004) is notable for its sheer narrative verve and keen political analysis. The most comprehensive scholarly biography currently available in English is Philip Dwyer's highly readable two-volume study *Napoleon: The Path to Power*, and *Citizen Emperor: Napoleon in Power* (New Haven, CT: Yale University Press, 2008 and 2013). In French, the standard biography for the early Napoleon is now Patrice Gueniffey's

Bonaparte, 1769–1802 (Paris: Gallimard, 2013), which appeared in English translation from Harvard University Press in 2015 (under the same title). Gueniffey plans to follow it in due course with *Napoléon, 1802–1821*. Among older biographies, a classic reference is Jean Tulard's Napoleon: *The Myth of the Saviour*, trans. Teresa Waugh (London: Weidenfeld and Nicolson, 1984).

The Age of the Napoleonic Wars

On the wars themselves, the classic survey in English remains David G. Chandler, *The Campaigns of Napoleon: The Mind and Method of History's Greatest Soldier* (New York: Scribners, 1966). A more recent survey, focusing on international relations, is Charles Esdaile, *Napoleon's Wars: An International History, 1803–1815* (London: Allen Lane, 2007). A broader study that places the wars within a cultural context is David A. Bell, *The First Total War: Napoleon's Europe and the Birth of Warfare As We Know It* (Boston: Houghton Mifflin, 2007). As for the larger diplomatic context, see, above all, Paul W. Schroeder's *The Transformation of European Politics, 1763–1848* (Oxford: Clarendon, 1994)—although keep in mind that Schroeder considers Napoleon a criminal for violations of international law. On the French military, Rafe Blaufarb, *The French Army 1750–1820: Careers, Talent, Merit* (Manchester: Manchester University Press, 2002), and Alan Forrest, *Napoleon's Men: The Soldiers of the Revolution and Empire* (London: Bloomsbury, 2006), provide excellent starting points. The most concerted publishing enterprise in English devoted to the wars in their broad context is Palgrave Macmillan's series *War, Culture and Society, 1750–1850*, edited by Rafe Blaufarb, Alan Forrest, and Karen Hagemann. A list of titles is available at http://www.unc.edu/wcs/.

Reference Works

In French, the standard work is still Jean Tulard, ed., *Dictionnaire Napoléon* (Paris: Fayard, 1989). Owen Connelly's *Historical Dictionary of Napoleonic France, 1799–1815*, 2 vols. (Westport, CT: Greenwood, 1985), focuses above all on military history. Also in French, the fascinating *Itinéraire de Napoléon au jour le jour*, by Jean Tulard and Louis Garros (Paris: Tallandier, 2002) provides information on literally every day of Napoleon's life. The websites www.napoleon-series.org and www.napoleon.org provide links to many online resources on the Napoleonic era, including those primary sources available on the Internet.

Primary Sources

Napoleon's life is one of the best documented in history. Of the virtual ocean of primary sources, the single most important is his extensive correspondence, of which a new, complete collection has been published: *Correspondance générale: Napoléon Bonaparte*, ed. Thierry Lentz et al., 15 vols. (Paris: Fayard, 2004–). A comprehensive list of memoirs from the period can be found in Jean Tulard et al., *Nouvelle bibliographie critique des mémoires sur l'époque napoléonienne écrits ou traduits en français* (Geneva: Droz, 1991). See also the websites listed in the previous section. Two excellent short document collections in English are Rafe Blaufarb and Claudia Liebeskind, *Napoleon: A Symbol for an Age* (Boston: Bedford/St. Martin's, 2007), and Rafe Blaufarb and Claudia Liebeskind, *Napoleonic Foot Soldiers and Civilians* (Boston: Bedford/St. Martin's, 2011).

Introduction

On eighteenth-century France and the Revolution, the best introduction in English is Colin Jones, *The Great Nation: France from Louis XV to Napoleon* (London: Allen Lane, 2002). See also William Doyle, *The French Revolution: A Very Short Introduction* (Oxford: Oxford University Press, 2001). On the revolutionary wars, the best survey remains T. C. W. Blanning, *The French Revolutionary Wars: 1787-1802* (London: Arnold, 1996).

Chapter 1: The Corsican, 1769–1796

On Napoleon's background and youth, see Dorothy Carrington, *Napoleon and His Parents: On the Threshold of History* (New York: Viking, 1988). Andy Martin's enjoyable *Napoleon the Novelist* (London: Polity, 2001), which discusses his lifelong literary ambitions, concentrates on the early years as well. Napoleon's early writings are available in the collection by Frédéric Masson and Guido Biagi, *Napoléon Inconnu: Papiers inédits, 1786-1793*, 2 vols. (Paris: Ollendorff, 1895).

Chapter 2: The general, 1796–1799

Beyond the material listed earlier on the wars, a good survey of Napoleon's first Italian campaign is Martin Boycott-Brown, *The Road to Rivoli: Napoleon's First Campaign* (London: Cassell, 2001). On the Egyptian campaign, see Juan Cole, *Napoleon's Egypt: Invading the Middle East* (Houndmills, UK: Palgrave Macmillan, 2007). On the background to the coup of the Eighteenth Brumaire, see Howard G. Brown's *Ending the French Revolution: Violence, Justice and Repression from the Terror to Napoleon* (Charlottesville: University of Virginia Press, 2006). The coup itself is covered in detail by Patrice Gueniffey, *Le dix-huit Brumaire: L'épilogue de la Révolution française, 9–10 novembre 1799* (Paris: Gallimard, 2008).

Chapter 3: The First Consul, 1799–1804

On Napoleon's domestic record, the most authoritative French survey is Jacques-Olivier Boudon, *Histoire du Consulat et de l'Empire, 1799–1815* (Paris: Perrin, 2000). Louis Bergeron's *France under Napoleon*, trans. R. R. Palmer (Princeton, NJ: Princeton University Press, 1981), remains highly useful. A particularly insightful study is Isser Woloch, *Napoleon and His Collaborators: The Making of a Dictatorship* (New York: Norton, 2001). Different perspectives on Napoleon's policies toward conquered territories can be found in Stuart Woolf, *Napoleon's Integration of Europe* (London: Routledge, 1991), and Michael Broers, *Europe Under Napoleon, 1799–1815* (London: Arnold, 1996). Broers provides a more in-depth look at the Italian case in *The Napoleonic Empire in Italy, 1796–1814: Cultural Imperialism in a European Context?* (Houndmills, UK: Palgrave Macmillan, 2005).

Chapter 4: The emperor, 1804–1812

In general, for the campaigns of the first years of the Empire, see the general histories listed earlier. But Christopher Duffy's *Austerlitz 1805* (Hamden, CT: Archon, 1977) remains a useful study of Napoleon's greatest battle. Charles Esdaile, *The Peninsular War: A New History* (Harmondsworth, UK: Penguin, 2003) provides a comprehensive survey of the war in Spain and Portugal, albeit from a highly Anglocentric viewpoint.

Chapter 5: Downfall, 1812–1815

Adam Zamoyski, *Moscow 1812: Napoleon's Fatal March* (New York: HarperCollins, 2004), provides a vivid overview of the Russian campaign and is usefully complemented by Dominic Lieven, *Russia Against Napoleon: The True Story of the Campaigns of War and Peace* (New York: Viking, 2010), written by the direct descendant of one of the Russian commanders. Michael Leggiere has a new, detailed study of the final military campaigns, *The Fall of Napoleon*, vol. 1, *The Allied Invasion of France, 1813–14* (Cambridge: Cambridge University Press, 2007). Munro Price's *Napoleon: The End of Glory* (Oxford: Oxford University Press, 2014) is excellent on Napoleon's last years in power and the Hundred Days. On Waterloo, see Andrew Roberts, *Waterloo, June 18, 1815: The Battle for Modern Europe* (New York: HarperCollins, 2005).

Epilogue: 1815–the present

Emmanuel de Las Cases's *Mémorial de Sainte-Hélène* is available in many free editions online. The original English translation of 1823 can be found at https://archive.org/details/memorialdesainte00lasc. A good general study of Napoleon's legacy is R. S. Alexander, *Napoleon* (London: Arnold, 2001); Sudhir Hazareesingh explores Napoleon's durable impact on French politics in *The Legend of Napoleon* (Cambridge: Granta, 2004). Pieter Geyl's classic study of historiography is *Napoleon, For and Against*, trans. Olive Renier (London: Jonathan Cape, 1949). Also discussed in the epilogue are Edward Said, *Orientalism* (New York: Vintage, 1978), Claude Ribbe, *Le crime de Napoléon* (Paris: Privé, 2005), and Lionel Jospin, *Le mal napoléonien* (Paris: Seuil, 2014). The most famous literary representations of Napoleon are found in Leo Tolstoy's *War and Peace*, and in Victor Hugo's poem "L'Expiation," originally published in the 1853 collection *Les châtiments* (The Punishments). Ralph Waldo Emerson's essay "Napoleon: The Man of the World," offers a wonderful prose portrait.

Index

Note: the numbers of pages that include figures are followed by an italicized *f*.

Napoleon